Rule Your World
Pat Francis

The Ultimate Secret

Keys to Seeing Your Dreams and
Desires Fulfilled

"Law of Creation"

D0826713

ENDORSEMENTS

When you read *The Ultimate Secret*, you will want to shout what is written here from every rooftop! In this book, Dr. Pat Francis takes the Law of Creation and shows each one how to mix their faith with power to fulfill the desire and destiny of God for their lives. Not only does Dr. Francis use the principles of God, but she develops within the reader a method of believing, seeing and receiving. Your heart will be filled with new power and joy as you learn the principles for making your dream a reality. *The Ultimate Secret* will help you understand FAITH, release the favor God and man in your life and reposition you for a new level of increase and success as you create your new world.

Dr. Chuck Pierce
Glory of Zion International Ministries Inc.

The Ultimate Secret is one of the most powerful books I have yet read explaining stage one, namely personal transformation. Your life will never count for something big unless you decide that you are going to do what it takes to experience your own transformation. If you are ready, the ultimate secret will activate in your life and launch you on the road to transformation. When this happens, there will be no doubt in your mind that your life can and will count for something really big!

C. Peter Wagner
Global Harvest Ministries

Dr. Pat Francis has given us truths in *The Ultimate Secret* to successful living and accomplishing great things. Those who procure the principles she presents will be empowered to prosper in every area of their life. Believers need to read this book and practice the principles presented until they become productive people in the Kingdom of God. Thanks Dr. Pat for blessing us with these simple biblical truths that will produce profound life transformation with incredible results.

Dr. Bill Hamon
Christian International Ministries Network

the *Ultimate* secret

Pat Francis

keys to seeing your dreams
and desires fulfilled

Belleville, Ontario, Canada

THE ULTIMATE SECRET
Copyright © 2009, Pat Francis

ISBN: 978-1-55452-351-1

**For more information or
to order additional copies, please contact:**
Pat Francis Ministries
info@patfrancis.org
1-877-668-5433

Guardian Books is an imprint of *Essence Publishing,* a Christian Book Publisher dedicated to furthering the work of Christ through the written word. For more information, contact:
20 Hanna Court, Belleville, Ontario, Canada K8P 5J2
Phone: 1-800-238-6376 • Fax: (613) 962-3055
E-mail: info@essence-publishing.com
Web site: www.essence-publishing.com

Printed in Canada
by

Guardian
B O O K S

DEDICATION

This book is dedicated to all the powerful people in the world.

You were created in the image and likeness of God. God made you with a divine design and the ability to dream and create. With the help of this book, you can create your new world, rule by what you say, and see your dreams and desires fulfilled.

For you created my inmost being; you knit me together in my mother's womb. I praise you because I am fearfully and wonderfully made; your works are wonderful, I know that full well (Psalm 139:13-14).

TABLE OF CONTENTS

(Special Appreciation)

ACKNOWLEDGEMENTS

Two are better than one, because they have a good return for their work (Ecclesiastes 4:9).

This book is yet another proof that nobody succeeds alone.

Thanks to the Lord Jesus Christ, for without His saving grace, strength, and continued help my life would be meaningless.

Thanks to my committed intercessors, family, pastors and staff, whose untiring prayers and encouragement have girded me with strength. You are my most treasured gifts from God.

FOREWORD

D o you want your life to count for something big: something bigger than yourself, your family or your present life. If you do, you have the right book in your hands.

Let me explain. It began in the Garden of Eden. When God created Adam and Eve, you and I were present. I know this may sound strange at first, but just think about it. No matter who you are, you have some of Adam's DNA and some of Eve's DNA. In fact, the Hebrew name *Adam* is also the word that means the whole human race. That is why, at least in terms of seed, you were part of creation way back then.

I love the way that Dr. Pat Francis draws out the implications of this in chapter after chapter throughout this book. She calls it the "Law of Creation." Once you understand the Law of Creation, you will be convinced that your life truly can count for something big.

For example, God told Adam and Eve that He created them so they could have dominion over all the rest of creation. They could have dominion over their personal lives, over their family, over their relationships, over their finances, over their health, over their work, over their play, and even over their communities and the society in which they live. All that potential is there for us as well, because each one of us is made in the image of God.

God expects His people, the Church, to transform society so it reflects the values and the virtues of the kingdom of God. That is well and good. But the Church will never be able to transform society unless and until the individuals, like you, who make up the Church are transformed themselves. Stage one is personal transformation. Then that opens the door for stage two, social transformation.

The Ultimate Secret is one of the most powerful books I have yet read explaining stage one, namely personal transformation. Your life will never count for something big unless you decide that you are going to do what it takes to experience your own transformation. Too many people waste time in prayer asking God to transform them one night and expect to wake up the next morning transformed. Or they go to a rousing church service on Sunday and expect that on Monday they will be transformed. What they don't understand is that even though God wants them transformed, He is not going to do it by Himself. He has created you with the ability to move into your own transformation by making the right choices because you are in His image.

I am sure that what I have just said is causing you to respond, "Yes, I do want to make the right choices, but how do I make them? I need help!" Pat Francis knows you need help, and that is why she has written *The Ultimate Secret*. Think of this book as a well from which you will draw fresh, life-giving water and drink. Draw up a bucket of faith, then a bucket of power, then a bucket of belief, then a bucket of confession, and finally a bucket of receiving. Do not hurry. Drink as deeply as you know how from each one.

When you do, *The Ultimate Secret* will activate in your life and launch you on the road to transformation. When this happens, there will be no doubt in your mind that your life can and will count for something really big!

C. Peter Wagner, Presiding Apostle
International Coalition of Apostles

PREFACE

Is there anything barren, worrisome, fearful and joy-eroding in your life? If so, you have the power to create your new world by applying the five principles of *The Ultimate Secret* that are unveiled in this book.

God has created you with great powers and abilities that are yet to be discovered. His Word declares that He made you in His image and in His likeness, which means that every person has the spiritual DNA of God. *"So God created man in his own image, in the image of God he created him; male and female he created them"* (Genesis 1:27). *"Then God said, 'Let us make man in our image, in our likeness, and let them rule"* (Genesis 1:26). Like God, you have the power of choice and the power to create. Like God, you are special with special powers and the ability to create your world.

Creating worlds of success in your family life, business, career, calling, etc., are possible using *The Ultimate Secret*, which applies the "Law of Creation." God, as Creator, created you in His image and likeness with the ability to also create your world. The world, as we know it, was created by mankind. The earth was created by God, but we created our world. The environmental issues and evil systems that systemically keep people in bondage are the result of man's creation.

You can create your new world, which is your areas of influence—family, relationships, business, career, ministry, finances, recreation, calling and purpose. Your world is who you are, what you do, who you know and where you live. Your areas of influence are yours to recreate using *The Ultimate Secret.*

God wants you to prosper. He led me to write this book to release the Law of Creation that will help you to begin to create and recreate a world with success as He intended for all mankind, based on the five principles of *The Ultimate Secret.* Instead of waiting for your desires to come by *chance,* you can create them by *choice* once you start exercising the Law of Creation and create your new world.

Reading this book is a start, but it is only a means to an end. You must apply what you learn. Once you apply the five principles of *The Ultimate Secret,* you will see your dreams and desires fulfilled.

INTRODUCTION

E veryone wants something. Most people want to accomplish some feat, yet seldom do. Whether you dream of simply owning a home or operating a great business, *everything* is possible to those who believe.

The Ultimate Secret is based on five principles: have faith, ask, believe, confess and receive. The key principle is that man was made in the image and likeness of God, Who, by the power of His spoken word, created the entire universe. This is the Law of Creation—to speak and create with words of faith.

Like God, man has the ability to control, affect change and influence his environment through what he believes and speaks into being.

It is the Law of Creation in action that will enable you to create your world and operate from your divine design. You were created in the image and likeness of God. God is spirit, therefore your activity in life must be spiritual as well as natural, emotional as well as strategic.

The Scriptural foundation for *The Ultimate Secret* is found in the New Testament book of Mark 11:12-14; 20-25, where Jesus cursed a fig tree for not bearing fruit. The next day, the Bible says, the tree had withered from its roots, something quite extraordinary for having only been blooming the day before. Jesus admonished

His disciples that what He had done to a fruitless tree they could also do.

The power of faith and the power to ask are essential principles of *The Ultimate Secret*. These principles are examined in very specific and practical ways. I urge you to be specific in "asking," therefore encouraging a communication with God that is candid and honest. Often, believers ask what they think God wants to hear and not necessarily what is on their heart. God, however, is all-knowing and desires honest communication from the heart.

The word *believe* is also critically examined. I explore the vast difference and correlation between belief and faith, portraying that belief is a pattern and process of thinking, while faith is a confidence that our desires are already a reality waiting for manifestation.

The power to confess and receive is also examined as this book coaches you into a new dimension of creating your new world.

I use storytelling, Bible stories and witty quotes to provide valuable insights that may have been overlooked in the past. At the end of each chapter is a series of points called "Pat's Points"— quick and easy recollections of what was discussed in the chapter.

Quite ironically, *The Ultimate Secret* is written to provide you with revelation knowledge of the Law of Creation as taught by Jesus Christ. This book makes The Ultimate Secret no secret at all.

Part One

POWER OF FAITH

"Faith is to believe what you do not see; the reward of this faith is to see what you believe."

Saint Augustine

One

I Can't Keep a Secret

You remember the times, as a child, when chubby hands gripped pint-sized ears in discretion. You placed your mouth close to the ear of your friend, your eyes bulging with newfound information. Oh, what a joy! Telling a secret! And you recall the astonished look your friend had when you revealed all you knew, giggling as though there wasn't a care in the world. And really, for you there wasn't. What was the secret? Oh, it could've been anything—didn't matter. Maybe you caught Jim and Suzy passing love notes in class, or you saw your teacher, Mrs. Llewellyn, sneaking in a snack when she thought none of you were looking. But you were king of the moment. You had a secret, and it was all yours to tell.

Well, my friend, today I have for you the ultimate secret, with its principles to seeing your dreams and desires fulfilled through the Law of Creation.

I have often wondered about people who look happy. People with great material wealth; people of high esteem and social status; people who seemed to be living their lives complete, maximizing their true potential and seeing their dreams come through. What caused their accomplishments? What created their inner drive? The journey to success is a road with obstacles,

19

disappointments and setbacks; nevertheless they seemed to overcome and achieve.

In my life, I've come to know the Lord Jesus Christ in a very intimate and personal way. During this time, He has shaped and inspired a series of teachings in me under the theme *"The Ultimate Secret"* as taught by His Word. The teachings are answers to my questions, and maybe that of yours, from long ago. In these teachings, the Lord revealed five major principles to seeing my desires fulfilled. I believe they will radically transform your life—if you use them. Here are the five principles of The Ultimate Secret as taught by Jesus Christ:

The Power of Faith
The Power to Ask
The Power to Believe
The Power to Confess
The Power to Receive

The Bible reveals The Ultimate Secret:

The next day as they were leaving Bethany, Jesus was hungry. Seeing in the distance a fig tree in leaf, he went to find out if it had any fruit. When he reached it, he found nothing but leaves, because it was not the season for figs. Then he said to the tree, "May no one ever eat fruit from you again." And his disciples heard him say it (Mark 11:12-14).

In the morning as they went along, they saw the fig tree withered from the roots. Peter remembered and said to Jesus, "Rabbi, look! The fig tree you cursed has withered!" "Have faith in God," Jesus answered. "I tell you the truth, if anyone of you says to this mountain, 'Go, throw yourself into the sea,' and does not doubt in his heart but believes that what he says will happen, it will be done for him. Therefore I tell you, whatever you ask for in prayer, believe that you have received it, and it will be yours" (Mark 11:20-24).

This particular passage generously lays the scope of *The Ultimate Secret,* as it is loaded with the Law of Creation and the five principles in creating your new world. You can have the desires of your heart. God wants you to have the desires of your heart. You have perhaps read many "how to" books, most of them claiming to be the ultimate "how to" book to success. Allow me to encourage you to take a notepad and a pen or pencil and take notes as you read *The Ultimate Secret* with its five principles to seeing your dreams and desires fulfilled through the Law of Creation.

Two

WHAT IS FAITH?

There's been a phenomenal growth in the interest of action heroes lately. The entertainment industry has capitalized on this interest, spawning a new wave of films, books, cartoons, even merchandise glorifying some hero who saved a little girl, a dying grandmother or a city. I'm always amazed at a particular factor consistent in every film, book, or TV program or the faith of a community in their action hero. The entire world could be going to shambles, science has failed, political figures have failed, and yet that community will hinge on the ability of its Superman, Spiderman or Batman, always believing "he will save us." Faith is a key ingredient to fiction characters.

THE FIRST PRINCIPLE OF THE ULTIMATE SECRET—
THE POWER OF FAITH

Jesus told His disciples, *"Have faith in God"* (Mark 11:22). Not only did He declare faith as a must, but He also warned them to be specific about *whom and what* they put their faith in. Everything we do in life is based on faith. Disappointments come when we put our faith in someone or in something that fails us. Faith in God will be discussed further. Since faith is a key factor, we will discuss the power of *faith* and your power of choice. What is faith?

Faith Is Confidence

The Bible says in Hebrews 11:1 that *"Faith is being sure of what we hope for and certain of what we do not see."* In other words, faith is confidence that our desires are already a reality in the realm of the unseen waiting for manifestation in the natural.

Another Bible translation says faith is *"the warranted deed for the thing which you have hoped for is at last yours."* In that case, faith is much like the deed you receive when you purchase a house or a piece of property. That deed proclaims that the property belongs to you and is now legally in your possession even before you move in. In the supernatural realm, faith has that same power. It is the confidence that you now possess what you hope for and have a certainty that you now receive what you do not yet see. Faith is the master key to unlocking the doors of your desires.

Hope is the Mother of Faith. *"Now faith is the substance of things hoped for"* (Hebrews 11:1, NKJV). Faith is "Now" a reality. Hope births faith. Your dream starts with a desire; then it becomes hope. Hope births faith and create miracles.

Dream ➤ Desire ➤ Hope ➤ Faith ➤ Miracle

Hope is the journey, and faith is the destination. Hope is future, and faith is now.

To adequately understand the true meaning and power of faith, you must understand that you operate in two realms—the natural and the supernatural. The natural realm is the seen realm. You operate in a realm of feeling, tasting, touching, seeing and hearing. The supernatural realm is the unseen realm and is just as real as the natural realm. It is a realm of the divine, the realm of the supernatural and the realm where God exists. Just as there are principles to live by in the seen realm, there are principles to follow to fully activate the benefits of the unseen realm. Faith is your ability to unlock the unseen realm and bring your unrealities into reality.

Faith Is Not a Feeling

Faith is not an emotion. It is not a feeling to turn on and off when you feel like it. Faith is a powerful constant that determines whether you will ever attain that desired goal or not. If faith is just a feeling, then our mood for the moment would determine the outcome of our desires. Think about the things that would or would not happen if faith was a mere feeling.

Noah Would Not Have Built the Ark

God told Noah to build an ark to protect His people from a severe flood at a time when there was no rain, never mind the possibility of having a flood. Noah believed God and began to build an ark that was designed by the Master Creator, a ship that proved greater than the Titanic (Genesis 6-9). Imagine all the criticism and hard work Noah endured while building that great big ark. His friends and family had never seen a flood and could not believe something beyond their experience. Imagine if Noah had thrown down his tools one day and said, "God, I'm tired and it really doesn't look like it's going to rain. Maybe the people are right. Maybe they are not being negative but just realistic. I quit!" His family would not have been saved and a new world would not have been restored after that historic flood thousands of years ago.

Moses Would Have Turned Back

Imagine the feelings of frustration, tiredness and weariness Moses endured during the time he led the Israelites, after numerous battles with Pharaoh, from Egyptian slavery into their freedom (Exodus 3-40). Imagine the burden of responsibility on his shoulders, with over two million people looking to him. Had Moses depended on his feelings, the Israelites may have never seen the Promised Land forty years later. Faith was not only present in Moses' life, but it was active, dynamic and encouraging him to move on even in the midst of opposition, criticism and his feelings.

ABRAHAM WOULD NOT HAVE OFFERED HIS SON

In Genesis chapter 22, God asked Abraham to sacrifice his son Isaac, a miracle child who was born to him and Sarah after many years of barrenness and struggle to have a child. Imagine the joy of receiving a child in your old age, and then being asked to sacrifice him! Imagine how you would have felt as you trotted up that mountain with your son, who, knowing that there would be a sacrifice, did not see a lamb. In verse 7, Isaac said to Abraham, *"Father?... The fire and wood are here...but where is the lamb for the burnt offering?"* Your response might have been through tears; maybe you would have turned back and said you simply could not do it. Or maybe, like Abraham, you would've strived with faith over feeling and attempt to obey God while trusting in His nature and power to work all things for His good and yours.

As the story goes, the Lord stopped Abraham just as he willingly raised the knife to slay his son. It was a test that proved to Abraham, our father of faith through whom God would birth and bless nations, his love for God and his commitment to his assignment and purpose.

The Lord declared to Abraham in verses 16 to 17, *"because you have done this and have not withheld your son, your only son, I will surely bless you and make your descendants as numerous as the stars in the sky and as the sand on the seashore."* And God did exactly as He promised.

The Lord tested Abraham, and Abraham believed God. The Bible says that because Abraham believed God it was credited to him as righteousness (in right standing with God for manifested promises) (Galatians 3:6). I wonder how many of us are living based on feeling, and failing all our tests, holding back the ultimate promises of God. Take a moment to examine yourself, and before you read on, ask yourself if there's anything in your life that you base your feelings on more than on your obedience and faith. What are your desires? How strong is your faith versus your feelings?

FAITH IS A TOOL

Faith is the instrument to obtaining your wildest dreams. According to Mark 5:24-34, there was a woman who suffered tremendously with a bleeding disorder for twelve years. She had visited many doctors. In today's world, that means she would have visited doctors from her hometown and overseas. Imagine the bills she would have incurred in travelling. Imagine the fatigue from her hemorrhaging and the discouragement she would have endured paying doctors for consultation, tests, medicine, all ending in the same results—nothing can be done. Few people would have dared her to go on; most may have implied that she should give up because her sickness was her fate. Who would have actually told her that she really and truly could be freed from her suffering?

Somehow this woman heard of Jesus, who had healed lepers and people with all kind of sickness and diseases. Hope came, and her faith was activated. She dared to believe once more. Her *faith was the key to her healing*. The Bible says that when she heard about Jesus, she came up behind him and touched his cloak, as she thought to herself, *"If I just touch his clothes, I will be healed."* As she reached out and grabbed the hem of his garment, she was *immediately* freed from her suffering as she felt warmth within her body, and she knew that she was *healed.*

In the midst of hundreds of people around him, Jesus felt that someone had activated his power through the instrument of faith and had received healing. He excitedly searched for that person, who knew a rare principle that he was still trying to teach his disciples. The woman fearfully came and fell at his feet, confessing that it was she who had touched him. Jesus said to her, *"Daughter, your faith has healed you. Go in peace and be freed from your suffering."*

I believe the woman did all that she could to be healed, and yet the main catalyst for her healing was *her faith,* coupled with the dynamic healing power of Jesus Christ. Faith was the tool she used to activate and release healing power into her body, soul and spirit! By calling her "daughter" Jesus gave her affirmation and acceptance. He gave her His peace, peace with God and peace in her soul. She had made divine connection and was restored to love of her Creator. She was freed from her suffering—physical, mental, emotional and spiritual. She was made whole.

A Lesson for Me

I took a group of volunteers to Nongoma, South Africa, to do a medical mission and work with children at risk. The king of the Zulu nation, His Majesty King Goodwill Zwelethini, invited us to hold a mission on the palace grounds. He hosted us for lunch, and as we shared together about the plight of the people in South Africa in their fight with disease and poverty, I was able to share my vision of creating solutions for children and people at risk by building orphanages and schools with an economic development plan to provide employment. My plan is to change from systemic poverty to systemic prosperity. Hence the projects that we do for people at risk will always have an education, employment and business component.

I asked His Majesty for land to build an orphanage for our first poverty reversal project in Africa.

Now, according to my level of faith and experience of working in various countries, I thought five to ten acres would be quite adequate. That was based on my belief system, which we will talk more about in chapter 7. Nevertheless I was convinced that five to ten acres would have been a generous donation.

The king arranged to give us some property, and I took our team to look at the beautiful property surrounded by hills in the picturesque Nongoma valley. One of our team members, Grantley, is a man of faith. I asked him how many acres he thought we should ask for. Grantley replied, "Pastor Pat, let us believe for one hundred acres." In my mind, I thought he was not being reasonable, but I didn't say it.

As we were perusing the land, my faith grew to believe for ten acres. I thought I was really growing in my journey of faith. However, to my amazement, the king decided that he would give us fifty acres of the most prized property in the valley of Nangoma!

Then the miracle happened. I knew the king had made a verbal commitment to give us fifty acres, but by the time His Majesty sent his letter confirming the gift, he doubled the amount and gave us one hundred acres, just like Grantley had said!

What happened?

Grantley's faith and his confession created a reality. I am reminded again of a statement of Jesus, *"All things are possible to him who believes"* (Mark 9:23, NKJV). You can have what you believe and create by what you say.

FAITH DOES NOT ASK FOR PERMISSION

Notice that neither Grantley nor I asked the king for one hundred acres of land. But one of us activated the power of faith. Likewise, the woman who had been hemorrhaging for twelve years did not personally ask Jesus to heal her. She simply heard that He could heal and thought to herself, "If I can touch Him, I can by my faith in His power pull a miracle of healing into my body." She knew a principle that very few ever learn—faith does not request permission. She knew that the power resided in Jesus Christ, and if she had access to that power, her healing would come. In the same manner, there is an abundance of wealth, prosperity, healing, and peace already provided for us through Christ dying on the cross. The Bible says Jesus was wounded for our transgressions and bruised for our iniquities; the chastisement of our peace is upon Him and by His stripes we *are* healed (Isaiah 53:5). This means everything we need to accomplish our purpose in this life is *already* provided! We just need the *faith* to access it!

Faith Is a Weapon

I am not speaking of physical weaponry but of spiritual weaponry—far more powerful than any tangible weapon. The apostle Paul admonishes us in Ephesians 6:16 to *"take up the shield of faith, with which you can extinguish all the flaming arrows of the evil one."* Just like the Roman shields were covered in leather and soaked in water so they could extinguish fiery arrows that were aim at the soldiers' hearts, the shield of faith is a spiritual weapon and covering used to extinguish the lies and suggestions of Satan. His arrows come in many forms to destroy hope and faith in our hearts—doubt, opposition, fear, intimidation, criticism, slander, depression, and rejection. The Bible urges us to use faith to withstand all these negative darts, meaning that when your faith is strong it becomes a spiritual shield and protective weapon for your soul.

Without Faith, You Cannot Please God

You can be lovable, educated, very kind, hospitable, a good wife or husband, a good student or teacher, a regular church attendee, give your tithe and volunteer at your favourite charity, and yet, the Bible says, *"without faith it is impossible to please God"* (Hebrews 11:6). It goes on to say that it's impossible because *"anyone who comes to him must believe that he exists and that he rewards those who earnestly seek him."*

Nothing gets the attention of God like faith. Let's look at the God-pleasing faith of the centurion in Matthew chapter 8.

> *When Jesus had entered Capernaum, a centurion came to him, asking for help. "Lord," he said, "my servant lies at home paralyzed and in terrible suffering." Jesus said to him, "I will go and heal him." The centurion replied, "Lord, I do not deserve to have you come under my roof. But just say the word, and my servant will be healed"* (Matthew 8:5-8).

What great faith! Here is a man with a paralyzed servant at home, suffering, and his request is only that Jesus would *send* the word of healing, and His powerful word carried into the air waves would reach his servant and create healing! This is the Law of Creation: to create by what we say. The centurion did not need Jesus to come to his house to touch his servant! He knew Jesus had the power to create as He spoke. That man took faith to another level. He had faith in creative words and not just faith in a healing touch. His faith pleased God, and faith that pleases God is the kind of faith that takes God at His word, believes it, and acts on it, knowing that He will do what He said. This was Jesus' reply:

> When Jesus heard this, he was astonished and said to those following him, "I tell you the truth, I have not found anyone in Israel with such great faith... Go! It will be done just as you believed it would." And his servant was healed at that very hour (Matthew 8:10,13).

Just as great faith pleases God, lack of faith displeases Him, as it negates the manifestation of His power. For years Jesus had lived in a town call Nazareth as a carpenter in business with His father, Joseph. Because of the people's familiarity with Him as a businessman, they did not accept Him when he started His ministry and manifestation as the Messiah. The man Jesus was also the Son of God. Jesus was the Christ, the Anointed One whose miracles and messages confirmed His anointing as identified in Mark 6:1-3:

> Jesus left there and went to his hometown, accompanied by his disciples. When the Sabbath came, he began to teach in the synagogue, and many who heard him were amazed. "Where did this man get these things?" they asked. "What's this wisdom that has been given him, that he even does miracles! Isn't this the carpenter? Isn't this Mary's son and the brother of James, Joseph, Judas and Simon? Aren't his sisters here with us?" And they took offense at him..

The Bible says that Jesus could not do any miracles there except lay hands on a few sick people and heal them, and he was amazed at their *lack of faith*.

Jesus said to them, "Only in his hometown, among his relatives and in his own house is a prophet without honor." He could not do any miracles there, except lay his hands on a few sick people and heal them. And he was amazed at their lack of faith (Mark 6:4-6).

When the Bible says that Jesus "could not" do any miracles there, it does not mean his power was suddenly weak. It means that without the presence of faith in a believer, the power of God remains inactive as only "potential." Energy can be categorized in two main classes: potential and kinetic energy. Kinetic energy is energy in motion, active energy. So faith activates the potential power of God from a state of rest to motion and activity, from "potential" to "kinetic" or active.

FAITH COMES BY HEARING

I am always in awe of the innocence of children. Have you ever noticed that whatever you tell them, they will believe? You tell them there's a Santa Claus, and they will stay awake all night on Christmas Eve waiting for him to arrive. You tell them the tooth fairy will come and replace a pulled tooth with a coin, and they will put that tooth under their pillow. You tell them there's a monster in the closet, and they will never open that door. What they hear, whether it is from a parent, teacher of friend, they will believe.

If you want to know exactly how your faith is built, reflect on how powerful media is and how it shapes what you believe. You may doubt what you hear the first time, but the more you hear it, the more you tend to believe it, even though initially you doubted what you heard at first. Verbal abuse is powerful because it is repetitive and creates realities in the mind of the hearer. This is *negative faith* that creates lies and deception for the purpose of destruction.

You can create positive faith. To strengthen your faith, take a page from a child's book. Perhaps this is one of the reasons Jesus says that to enter the kingdom of God we must become like little children (Mark 10:15). Believe in God and His Word. Strengthen your faith by reading and listening to the Word of God. Romans 10:17 tells us that our faith comes and continues to grow as we hear the Word of God. There are many ways to increase your faith using the Word of God:

- Have a daily time of devotion with God. Pray and read His Word.
- Read the Word of God out loud.
- Listen to teaching tapes.
- Watch faith-based programs.
- Listen to music based on the Word of God.
- Daily confess the Word of God over your life, family, career, business, etc.

It is said that if you listen to a teaching or a certain principle seven times, it will become a part of you. That is why you must be careful about what you hear and keep on hearing. What you hear, you can become.

There are also many ways to hinder your faith. Entertaining doubtful friends and family can be hazardous to your dreams. If faith comes through hearing, then you should monitor what you hear. Here are a few things to watch:

- Beware of negative people. They tend to drain energy and negate aspirations.
- Beware of books that are negatively inspired.
- Beware of TV programs or movies that can negatively affect you.
- Watch the news strategically, so as not to weaken your faith.
- Don't ignore the realities of today's society. Listen and learn with a guarded heart to preserve your soul from seeds of negativity that erodes faith.

* Protect your heart; the Bible says it is the *"wellspring of life"* (Proverbs 4:23).

HAVE FAITH IN GOD

When you put your faith in Jesus Christ, it creates a supernatural reality called salvation. The word *salvation* is all inclusive, with peace, safety, security, prosperity, provision and protection that come from a relationship with God. When you have faith in God, He saves you by becoming your Source of strength, power, provision, peace and protection. He becomes the Guide to your ultimate purpose with your permission.

Faith is so powerful that according to the Bible, we are *saved* through it. *"For it is by grace you have been saved, through faith—and this not from yourselves, it is the gift of God—not by works, so that no one can boast"* (Ephesians 2:8-9). How God expresses His love for the world is told in John 3:16: *"For God so loved the world that he gave his one and only Son, that whoever believes in him shall not perish but have eternal life."*

The word *perish* comes from the root word *per*, which means "through, completely, to destruction." The word *parallel* comes from the root word *para*, which means "beside" (*Online Etymology Dictionary*, www.etymonline.com). Parallel lines can never meet. To live a life parallel to your destiny is to live a life in vain. We are all born with gifts, talents and a specific calling and destiny. With God as our source, His leading, guiding and correcting will help us to live a life of purpose and power.

When we put out faith in God, our confession of our faith seals our positioning in Him. The Bible says in Romans 10:9-10:

> *If you confess with your mouth, "Jesus is Lord," and believe in your heart that God raised him from the dead, you will be saved. For it is with your heart that you believe and are justified, and it is with your mouth that you confess and are saved. As the Scripture says, "Anyone who trusts in him will never be put to shame."*

We see here that faith with confession secures our salvation and relationship with God. Let us have faith in God, pray and confess together:

Dear God, I believe in you and your Son Jesus Christ. I ask you to secure my salvation by activating my spirit with the Spirit of Christ as I confess my faith in you. I ask your forgiveness for all my weaknesses and wrong behaviour. Forgive me and bless me to fulfill my dreams and destiny for the purpose I was created. I confess that I am a child of God. I believe in you.

In Jesus' Name, Amen.

PAT'S POINTS

- Faith moves your impossibilities into the realm of possibilities.
- Faith is an intangible substance that brings tangible results.
- Faith is the primary tool used in manifesting your dreams.
- Faith is a powerful weapon.
- It is impossible to please God without faith.
- Have faith in God to combine the supernatural with your natural.
- Your connection with God is based on faith.
- Have faith in yourself.
- Faith is the first key to The Ultimate Secret.

Faith hears the inaudible, sees the invisible, believes the incredible, and receives the impossible.

Anonymous

Three

POWER OF FAITH, VISION, VISUALIZATION

You have probably heard the saying "Whatever the mind of man can conceive and believe, it can achieve" (Napoleon Hill). There are two principles at work in this quotation: the principle of "conception" and the principle of "belief." We have discussed what faith is; now let's delve into the power of a concept or vision, the basis of your desire.

Vision is so powerful and universal that many people have either lived or died because of someone's misuse of it. Governments, religious leaders, activists, other leaders and authorities make fundamental decisions based on their visions.

I can name countless persons who spoke and lived out their visions. Dr. Martin Luther King Jr. envisioned a world where people of all races would one day be united and not judged by the "color of their skin but by the content of their character." Adolf Hitler also had vision. He envisioned a nation of pure Anglo people, a nation, and eventually a world, of unmixed Germans. Both men had vision and both pursued their vision. They impacted society. But only one of those visions obviously benefited the entire world. Both began with an idea, a thought, an imagination.

Vision, like faith, is also intangible. It is a dynamic that shapes the dreams and goals of thousands. It is another key to the fulfillment of your desires. Vision is the precursor to your actual pursuit.

A WILD IMAGINATION

How wild is your imagination? What do you dare to dream? Envision it. Get in a comfortable sitting position and pull from your memory some of the things you wanted to do since you were a child. Do you remember them? Do you see them? Picture yourself doing exactly what you see. Is it within your grasp? Is it within your reach? Maybe there are goals that you set last year and did not accomplish. Picture yourself accomplishing them. Picture yourself making the necessary sacrifices it will take to achieve them. Picture yourself fulfilling them. What you picture begin to create by writing it down, setting goals and speaking what you saw.

I love a child's imagination. Children are not afraid to picture or imagine the wildest of events. But a great imagination, or the power to visualize, does not rest only with children. God has given *everyone* the gift of imagination. That means everyone can chart a course for his or her life. Anyone can visualize what they would like to see happen in the next five, ten or twenty years.

Genesis chapter 11 gives a fascinating account of imagination at work. It speaks about the Tower of Babel. A group of radical faith people came together to build a city with a tower that could reach the heavens. Zealous and overambitious, their purpose was to make a name for themselves excluding God. Their approach and motive was egotistical and proud, so God said, *"If as one people speaking the same language they have begun to do this, then nothing they plan [imagine] to do will be impossible for them"* (Genesis 11:6). In this event, God affirms the power of a dream mixed with imagination, faith and determination. It shows that *nothing is impossible to people of faith* in a culture of unity and passion.

JESUS AND VISION

During His time on earth, Jesus had great vision. His vision was to fulfill His mission, which was to save the world and restore people into relationship with God as their Father. During one of

Jesus' teaching, as thousands pressed in to hear Him speak, the people became hungry. His disciples' solution was to send the people away to get their own food. Jesus had a different solution—feed them. A little boy volunteered his lunch which was five loaves of bread and two fishes (Mark chapter 6). Jesus, by faith, told the crowd to sit in groups. He prayed, believed and acted on His faith. The lunch multiplied, and He was able to feed over 5,000 people with much left over. *Faith sees and faith acts to produce what it sees.*

JESUS ENDURED THE CROSS

What was Jesus *seeing* as He envisioned the journey to Calvary? The Bible says in Hebrews 12:2, *"who for the joy set before him endured the cross, scorning its shame, and sat down at the right hand of the throne of God."* Was Jesus envisioning the spikes that were to pierce His wrists? Was He envisioning the spear that would plunge into His side? He knew these things would happen, but this was not the picture that urged Him on to completion. He was urged on by a *vision*, because the Scripture says, *"the joy set before him.'* Jesus was picturing His resurrection! He was far beyond the cross. He envisioned Himself once again in heaven with His Father and the redemptive plan completed! He envisioned you and me in relationship with God conquering every obstacle to our purpose in life and pressing through to greater and greater achievements. You were already in the heart of God before you came to know Him.

The *purpose* of the cross gave Jesus joy and strength to endure it. Vision is what you see with spiritual eyes that gives hope and strength to endure the present, as your spiritual realities become more powerful than your natural realities.

YOUR VISION

Merely envisioning a dream is not enough. You must do something to accomplish it. Habakkuk 2:2 says, *"Write down the revelation [vision] and make it plain."* Begin to recognize a "good" idea versus a "God" idea. A good idea flutters into your brain and back out again. A God idea comes as a vision and stays with you consistently. It is the idea that you should take the time to seriously write down.

You must chart:

* What you see.
* How you will accomplish what you see.
* When you will accomplish what you see.
* Where you will accomplish what you see.
* Why you want to accomplish what you see.
* Who will be needed to help you accomplish what you see.
* The purpose for what you see.

A poem by C. W. Longenecker says it well:

You Can If You Think You Can!

If you think you are beaten, you are,
If you think you dare not, you don't.
If you like to win, but you think you can't,
It is almost certain you won't.
If you think you'll lose, you're lost,
For out in the world we find
Success begins with a fellow's will.
It's all in the state of mind.
If you think you are outclassed, you are,
You've got to think high to rise,
You've got to be sure of yourself before
You can ever win a prize.
Life's battles don't always go
To the stronger or faster man.
But soon or late the man who wins
Is the man who thinks he can.

The Bible says, *"As [a man] thinks in his heart, so is he"* (Proverbs 23:7, NKJV). This tells me that whether I think good or bad, whatever it is I think, imagine or envision, that is who I am.

VISION MISUSE

We talked about the power of vision in the lives of Dr. Martin Luther King Jr. and Adolf Hitler. Hitler misused the gift of imagination and created an evil imagination. In the same way, you can misuse your imaginative abilities to the detriment of yourself and others. The Bible calls it *"vain in their imaginations"* (Romans 1:21, KJV) as they worked against God's will.

Vain imaginations are unfruitful time wasters, and if misused they create negative or evil power. A serial killer uses vain imaginations to create an evil mind with evil power to destroy others.

Let us make a new commitment right now to discipline our thought life so we will only entertain positive imaginations, receive "God ideas" and create positive solutions.

GREAT IMAGINATIONS

Here are some inspirations from people with great imaginations.

- The Wright Brothers: self-taught engineers who used their imaginations to invent the first working airplane.
- Thomas Edison: famous for inventing the light bulb. This inventor used his imagination to patent over 1,000 inventions.
- Mary Anderson: known for holding the patent to windshield wipers in 1905.
- Rev. Dr. Billy Graham: famous evangelist, envisioned millions coming to know Jesus Christ as their personal Lord and Saviour.
- **You:** _____

Your vision may never make you famous. But it is important and should be pursued with everything within you.

PROTECTING YOUR VISION

You must believe that there is much negativity waiting to crush your vision. That negativity can come from family, friends and strangers or from your own vain imaginations. It is, therefore, imperative that you protect your vision, so the flame will never cease. Here's how:

* Prayer: Nurture your vision with prayer.
* Faith: Feed your vision with faith.
* Resist: Resist (active discipline) negative thoughts.
* Meditate: Meditate on the positive things and on the Word of God.
* Avoid: Avoid negative people.
* Strategy: Strategically share your vision only with people who will support you.
* Write: Write your vision. Writing your vision is most important. You need to be reminded by thinking it and by seeing it.
* Work: Work your vision. Do something every day to see your vision manifest.

The more you dare to dream, the bigger your dreams will become. Your imagination is infinite; it can go on and on and on. As you write your vision, do not let fear creep in. Do not think that you are too young, too old, too skinny, too fat, too anything to accomplish your vision. Remember that it is God who has given you the power to dream. *You* must dare to do it!

Four

HAVE FAITH IN GOD

F aith in someone is based on the character of that person. You put faith in someone because of their proven character. You put faith in something because of its history or because of your past experiences. By faith, you go to the sitting room and sit on a chair without first checking to see whether the screws were removed. You have faith in yourself because you know what you are capable of.

So faith in the spiritual world must be specific and directive. When you reach out to the spirit world, be specific about the God you choose to believe in, pray to, and have communion with. Radio waves carry music to your radio and signals to your TV or cellular telephone. You have a choice as to which channel to listen to or watch. Likewise, you must choose your spiritual connection to God through His Son, Jesus Christ. He is your connection to your Heavenly Father.

The Bible says, *"For there is one God and one mediator between God and men, the man Christ Jesus, who gave himself as a ransom for all men—the testimony given in its proper time"* (1 Timothy 2:5-6). Jesus Christ is the ultimate sacrifice and proof of God's great love for all mankind, including you. The Law of Cause and Effect states that all human beings are responsible for their actions. Every mistake has repercussions. Through Jesus Christ comes a more powerful law—the Law of Forgiveness. His punishment on the cross was for the freedom of all mankind regardless of culture, race and wrong behaviour of the past. He was punished for our sins. True repentance and faith in Jesus Christ brings life to the soul and restoration with God. With His Law of Forgiveness comes His peace to the soul and oneness with God.

Having faith in God is key to obtaining your deepest desires and dreams. You can have faith in God because of His character, His consistency and the proven testimony of His relationship with mankind throughout the ages.

I think about God as I write this, and I realize His attributes make us secure when our faith is in Him. God is:

* Love

    Whoever does not love does not know God, because God is love (1 John 4:8).

* Unchanging

    Jesus Christ is the same yesterday and today and forever (Hebrews 13:8).

* Almighty

    I am the Alpha and the Omega," says the Lord God, "who is, and who was, and who is to come, the Almighty" (Revelation 1:8).

* Peace

    And he will be called Wonderful Counselor, Mighty God, Everlasting Father, Prince of Peace (Isaiah 9:6).

* Faithful and True

    I saw heaven standing open and there before me was a white horse, whose rider is called Faithful and True (Revelation 19:11).

- Redeemer

  With everlasting kindness I will have compassion on you,"
  says the LORD your Redeemer (Isaiah 54:8).

- Father to the Fatherless

  A father to the fatherless, a defender of widows, is God in his
  holy dwelling (Psalm 68:5).

- A Friend

  "I no longer call you servants, because a servant does not
  know his master's business. Instead, I have called you friends,
  for everything that I learned from my Father I have made
  known to you" (John 15:15).

- Provider and Protector

  My God will meet all your needs according to his glorious
  riches in Christ Jesus (Philippians 4:19).

If that is not enough, here are just a few practical reasons why you should put your faith in God:

1. God Loves You!

The Bible says, *"But God demonstrates his own love for us in this: While we were still sinners, Christ died for us"* (Romans 5:8). Love is not just a feeling. It demands expression and action. Jesus Christ died on the cross a cruel death for imperfect people, which proves His love for you. He is not looking for perfect people to love. No one is perfect. His love reaches out to all the people of the world regardless of culture, race and experiences. God is love.

To have faith in God is to surrender to His love. That is the ultimate security and the key to true peace. He will be the only constant, unchanging person in your life. Neither death nor anything in this life can separate you from His love (Romans 8:35-39).

Death separates a husband and wife, families and friends. In Christ, you will live forever in His presence.

Some find it hard to believe in and accept the love of God. They feel unworthy because of imperfections. They find it hard to believe for kindness, favour and grace from God. The Bible says, *"Delight yourself in the Lord and he will give you the desires of your heart"* (Psalm 37:4). God wants you to delight in Him and not be afraid of Him. You must find complete contentedness with Him. He desires a relationship that has a win-win factor. He also wants to delight in you.

God created you to be in communion (common union) with Him. While He is a Master Provider and can give you all you would ever need, His primary goal is to be in fellowship with you. If you would take the time to "delight" yourself in Him, spend time with Him and worship Him, you will find that some of the things you have not even asked for yet are already provided!

2. God is a God of His Word

In the book of Genesis, we read the story of Abraham and Sarah, a married couple who were childless. God, however, called Abraham into a life of purpose that included an heir and to become *"the father of many nations"* (Genesis 17:4), the patriarch of billions of people. Abraham's wife, Sarah, however, was far beyond childbearing age. This idea was so far off for Abraham that when God told him he would bless him with a son he laughed to himself (Genesis 17:17), and so did Sarah (Genesis 18:12).

Have you ever told someone you would do something and they doubted you? How did it make you feel? It never feels good when people do not believe in you.

Nevertheless, God did not change His mind regarding His promise, even though doubt was present. The Bible says that *"God is not a man, that he should lie, nor a son of man, that he should change his mind"* (Numbers 23:19). Simply put, God is not like us.

Sometimes we are swayed by feelings, instincts, emotions and compulsion. God is not like that at all. If He says He will do a particular thing at a particular time, then you count it done! *"I will surely return to you about this time next year, and Sarah your wife will have a son,"* said God to Abraham (Genesis 18:10). The following year, around the same time that God had promised, Sarah gave birth to Isaac, the promised offspring. The Bible puts it this way: *"Now the Lord was gracious to Sarah as he had said"* (Genesis 21:1). It really is comforting to know that the God we are putting our faith in is not limited by emotions, circumstances or physical conditions. Sarah was at least ninety years old when she gave birth to Isaac.

Sometimes we think that God has a human memory. We know He said that He would prosper us and that He has good plans for us. We know He made certain promises to us, but after a year, maybe two years have passed, we think that God has *forgotten* us. Yet, Jesus reminds us in Luke 12:6-7, *"Are not five sparrows sold for two pennies? Yet not one of them is forgotten by God. Indeed, the very hairs of your head are all numbered. Don't be afraid; you are worth more than many sparrows."*

3. God Works Miracles

Think of the magic of that foot, comparatively small, upon which your whole weight rests. It's a miracle, and the dance...is a celebration of that miracle.

Martha Washington

Miracles are all around you. Breathe in, and breathe out. The breath of life is a miracle. Take a moment to peer outside, and you will see the miracle of nature. Witness the birth of a child, and you will appreciate the value of a miracle.

A miracle is an event, a happening of something inexplicable to the laws of nature. Based on the Bible, creation itself is a series of miracles worked by God in just a matter of days. Thousands of years later, miracles are still happening.

Jesus was known for many things, among them being a *miracle worker*. Earlier we disclosed the miracle of healing in the woman with a hemorrhaging problem. Space will not even allow me to elaborate on the many miracles Jesus performed, but here are a few:

- He gave a blind man sight (Luke 18:35-43).
- He raised a girl from the dead (Mark 5:21-43).
- He fed over 5,000 people with five loaves of bread and two fish (John 6:1-15).
- He raised from the dead a man called Lazarus, who had been in the grave for four days (John 11:38-44).
- He healed a deaf and mute man (Mark 7:31-37).
- He healed a crippled woman (Luke 13:11-13).
- He healed a man's daughter who was dying (Mark 5:37-43).
- He turned water into wine (John 2:1-11).
- He helped the disciples with a miraculous catch of fish (Luke 5:1-11).

It is clear that Jesus healed and blessed a lot of people, but you may ask what does that have to do with you, your family or your finances? God cares about *every* thing that concerns you, including your financial, emotional and spiritual circumstance. First Kings 17:8-16 gives us this insight:

> *Then the word of the LORD came to him [Elijah]: "Go at once to Zarephath of Sidon and stay there. I have commanded a widow in that place to supply you with food." So he went to Zarephath. When he came to the town gate, a widow was there gathering sticks. He called to her and asked, "Would you bring me a little water in a jar so I may have a drink?" As she was going to get it, he called, "And bring me, please, a piece of bread." "As surely as the LORD your God lives," she replied, "I don't have any bread—only a handful of flour in a jar and a little oil in a jug. I am gathering a few sticks to take home and make a meal for myself and my son,*

that we may eat it—and die." Elijah said to her, "Don't be afraid. Go home and do as you have said. But first make a small cake of bread for me from what you have and bring it to me, and then make something for yourself and your son. For this is what the LORD, the God of Israel, says: 'The jar of flour will not be used up and the jug of oil will not run dry until the day the LORD gives rain on the land.'" She went away and did as Elijah had told her. So there was food every day for Elijah and for the woman and her family. For the jar of flour was not used up and the jug of oil did not run dry, in keeping with the word of the LORD spoken by Elijah.

We see here a number of principles. First, God cares for the poor and works financial miracles. The widow was suffering at the hand of poverty when the man of God came to her and asked for water and a piece of bread. She may have thought that God had forgotten her, indeed she thought the bread she had would be her last on earth, but God distinctly sent Elijah to her. In fact, God had already planned two things at once:

1) He provided for Elijah in Zarephath through the giving of the woman, and
2) He provided for the woman through her obedience to the Word of God as spoken by the prophet Elijah.

I often wonder how many of the "coincidences" in our lives are really "God-incidences." When the widow went to gather sticks and found Elijah there, she may have thought it a coincidence, just her luck, that a man of God was there at the same time. Yet, the Lord had moved upon her to go to that place to gather those sticks. I call that a divine connection for a miracle opportunity.

Here is another principle in this miracle: God will release what He has *for* you if you will release what you have *to* Him. Imagine the widow telling a friend about Elijah asking her to sow into him and his anointing the last bit of food she has for her and her son, and her friend saying to her, "Are you crazy? You better keep that food for yourself! That man doesn't care about you or your family. He only came to take your last little bite to eat!" Even if she did not mention it to anyone, imagine the thoughts that ran through her mind. Imagine the thoughts that would race through your mind if you were in her position. Some of us are in her position today. Sometimes God requires us to first give in order to receive. It is called The Law of Sowing and Reaping. We sow to reap and give to receive.

When you are in a place of need, God will always move you to step out in faith and give what you have to yield a greater return tomorrow. If the widow had held on to her last meal, that is exactly what it would have been—her last meal. Instead, she stepped out in faith and gave first and thus yielded a greater return in the end. It is said, "The Lord does not ask more than he promises to give." He asked Abraham for his son Isaac, and Abraham in turn received a nation.

Does God still work miracles today? The Bible describes God as unchanging. He is the same *"yesterday and today and forever"* (Hebrews 13:8). That means his character and abilities do not change. He is still a miracle-working God. And the good news is, He *"is no respecter of persons"* (Acts 10:34, KJV), which means that if He can work a miracle for others, He can certainly work a miracle for you. Remember what we discussed before: God *wants* you to prosper, He *wants* you to be in good health, and He *wants* the best for you. Potential.

Here is God, who is not limited by our own abilities. When God summoned Moses and gave him the assignment of leading the Israelites out of Egypt, Moses focused on his own inabilities to do the job. Moses had a speech impediment, a murder record and was a fugitive trying to survive. Moses questioned God, asking *"Who am I, that I should go to Pharaoh and bring the Israelites out of Egypt?"* (Exodus 3:11).

God had already predestined Moses to be the deliverer of the Israelite nation. From the time of his birth, Moses was protected by God when His mother, by faith, placed him in a basket in the Nile River to protect him from being killed by Pharaoh (Exodus 2:3). Imagine God divinely protecting you from birth for a specific purpose. He is. God is working in our lives before we become aware of Him. God led you to read this book because He is nurturing you for the miraculous.

Miracles are divinely wrought by the Lord. Yet, it is our faith in God and our ability to receive from Him that will put us in a position to receive supernatural blessings. The Lord not only wants to work miracles *for* us; He wants to do miracles *through* us. He desires to be glorified in every area of our lives in spite of our inabilities, past mistakes or fears. If we put our faith in God who can do all things, He will release the power to manifest miracles in our lives.

The Bible says that God is able to do *"immeasurably more than all we ask or imagine, according to his power that is at work within us"* (Ephesians 3:20). God's power and ability to change your circumstance is not only *on* you but also *within* you when you put your faith in Him.

Here are some other traits of God that will encourage you to trust Him.

God is omnipotent (unlimited power, the almighty God).
God is omniscient (all knowing).
God is omnipresent (everywhere).

Building your faith in God is a daily process. As you read and hear His Word, your faith will grow. You will begin to recognize the miracles that you have already experienced, for God has been watching over you and working on your behalf. More miracles are yet to come by the power of faith that works in you. By your faith in God, you will have the ability to create your world by applying The Ultimate Secret.

PAT'S POINTS

As you grow in faith, remember:

- Have faith in God.
- God loves you.
- God wants you to prosper.
- God will perform His Word.
- God works miracles.
- Thank Him for past miracles.
- Expect a miracle every day.
- You are a miracle.
- Be thankful every day.
- By faith you can create your world.

Five

FAITH WORKS

aith not only works as it pertains to being one of the necessary tools for success, but it works (labours, moves, can be
set in motion, creates, is active). You display your faith by
what you do and by what you say. An *attitude* of faith must be cul-
tivated. The Bible calls it a "spirit of faith" (2 Corinthians 4:13).

A SPIRIT OF FAITH

The word *spirit* refers to attitude, passion, commitment, conversation and positioning. The Bible says, *"It is written: 'I
believed; therefore have I spoken.' With that same spirit of faith we
also believe and therefore speak"* (2 Corinthians 4:13). I'm sure you
have heard the saying "Your attitude determines your altitude."
How true. Some people can have a negative spirit. They will
always see the cup half empty. A negative spirit or a positive spirit
is strategically nurtured. Tiger Woods tells of how his father created and nurtured in him a positive and winning spirit.

A *spirit of faith* allows you to be an agent of change. Your out-
look on life is optimistic, and therefore when you enter a room or
a business meeting or even when you are just having fun, you are
creating a positive atmosphere around you. If you have ever been
around a pessimist, then you understand the power of a negative
spirit. A person with a negative spirit can crush your dreams as

one moment with them can leave you impregnated with fear and discouragement. With the spirit of faith, you have the ability to influence and positively affect others. You create a positive atmosphere. You develop a winning personality.

A spirit of faith dissipates fear. The Bible says, *"God has not given us a spirit of fear, but of power and of love and of a sound mind"* (2 Timothy 1:7, NKJV). The spirit of faith destroys negative thoughts of fear, depression and discouragement and will protect you from negativity from others.

In the Bible, there is a story about Jesus walking on the water as He approached the disciples in a boat. When they saw Him walking on the lake,

> *When the disciples saw him walking on the lake, they were terrified. "It's a ghost," they said, and cried out in fear. But Jesus immediately said to them: "Take courage! It is I. Don't be afraid." "Lord, if it's you," Peter replied, "tell me to come to you on the water." "Come," he said* (Matthew 14:26-29).

Peter got out of the boat and walked on water towards Jesus. Peter had faith to begin, but not enough faith to endure to the end. He looked at the circumstances around him and saw the rising waves. He listened to fear and heard the howling wind. Peter became *afraid*. He lost his faith and began to drown. He called out to Jesus as he was going down into the water. Jesus reached out his hand, caught him and said to Peter, *"You of little faith...why did you doubt?"* (Matthew 14:31).

Peter's spirit of faith made him walk on water. The power that made him step out and walk on water was also there to keep him to the end, the power within connecting with the power of God. You must guard your heart when you step out or take a risk to accomplish your dream. Things can get rough after you boldly step out. But you must nurture your spirit of faith and keep your faith alive to keep the dream alive. You must keep your focus on God, who will make the impossible

possible. Don't lose your spirit of faith. Keep walking with your eyes on God.

THREE KINDS OF PEOPLE

Based on the above story, that there are three kinds of people in the world:

1) People who dare to walk on water—the risk-takers.
2) People who sink because they could not endure—the fluctuaters.
3) People who never step out of the boat—the safe-but-sorriers.

You must dare to dream, dare to step out and keep your faith alive no matter what. The risk-takers are not foolish people. They are people like Peter. These people are well aware of all the odds against them. In business, they have done their research and know the reasons why their stepping out of the boat may not make any *present* sense. Yet they do it anyway. Why? Because what is outside of the boat is worth the risk. It is a life of continuous discovery. It is living the Law of Creation. These people are the risk-takers. They are faith-in-action people. They are not standing on the boat saying that they have faith yet never stepping out to try walking on water. Not only are they stepping out of their safe boat, experience and environment, but they are like Jesus encouraging others and saying "Come. You too can walk on water." When the world gives them the impossibilities, they show the possibilities. When they are handed problems, they create solutions. When life throws them a lemon, they create lemonade. They learn from mistakes and keep trying. Their failures become stepping stones to obtaining their dreams.

The fluctuaters are also risk-takers. They may tend to be spontaneous and open to new ideas, revolutions and methods of thinking. So they step out of the boat but do not take into account the amount of faith needed, not only to take them out of the boat but keep them continuously above the water. The journey destroyed their initial faith. They walk on the water without strength and endurance when trials come. In the midst of the overwhelming storm, they sometimes forget why they stepped out in the first place. They allow the setbacks, the disappointments in their journey to destroy their faith and purpose.

Stepping out is never enough. We must *"fight the good fight of faith."* God teaches us in His Word to *"Fight the good fight of faith. Take hold of the eternal life to which you were called when you made your good confession in the presence of many witnesses"* (1 Timothy 6:12).

Maintaining your faith is a fight because doubt and fear will surely come. Remember to encourage yourself and *daily* strengthen your faith by the positive words that you hear on the inside of your own mind and from outside influences. Speak faith. Listen to positive people and meditate on positive affirmation and on the Word of God.

The safe-but-sorriers never really experience what it is to either walk on water or sink. They are safe but sorry. They go through life without truly living a full life. They not only refuse to believe God for anything, but they refuse to do anything worth believing for. These people never develop the measure of faith that God wants to give them. In business, relationships, family and social life, these are the people who are content with safe mediocrity. They are spectators, people on the sideline looking at the fluctuaters and saying, "I told you not to step out of the boat," and saying the risk-takers, "It works for you but would never work for me. I like to play it safe."

Which person are you?

Both the fluctuaters and the safe-but-sorriers can become risk-takers.

The fluctuaters need to strengthen their faith, learn from their mistakes and dare to try again. They must learn to overcome fear and to see failure as a only school in the journey of their success and greater achievements.

The safe-but-sorriers must first be stirred to have faith to believe that they too can accomplish their dreams. It is an awakening and a realization that greater achievements are not only for others but available to all who dare to dream, dare to believe and dare to step out in spite of the risk. They must revisit their belief system and make necessary changes to believe in themselves and the love and power of God that will work in and through them.

We are not called to scientifically explain why we can walk on water, why the odds worked in our favour, why a marriage can be restored after adultery, why a divine connection with a special person changed our lives. God calls us to a greater life of faith. Faith is a journey and never a destination. Have faith in yourself. Have faith in God.

LIVING BY FAITH

Faith must become a lifestyle. The Bible encourages us to live by faith, trusting in God for even the simplest of desires. Here's how you can operate by faith:

- Name your desire.
- Pray to God for His divine intervention.
- See it done (remember the power of visualization).
- Confess its manifestation.
- Do what it takes in the natural.
- Expect your vision to materialize.
- Encourage yourself with words of faith.

It takes a lot of faith to *do* something that God tells you to do, but it takes even more faith to *wait* on God's timing. You can lose out on the miracles God has for you if you do not have enough faith to *wait on him*. Abraham and Sarah, after God promised them a child, did not have the patience to wait on God. They decided to take matters into their own hands. Sarah encouraged Abraham to sleep with their servant Hagar and impregnate her so she would have the son they always wanted.

The end result was pain and heartaches as Hagar later mocked Sarah's inability to have children. God did deliver on His promise, as we see in reading the entire account, but Sarah brought unnecessary pain on herself and upon her marriage when she did not wait on God and compromised the beauty of the promise (Genesis 16 and 17).

FAITH WORKS!

Faith is active, not passive. Action follows faith. Inaction is the result of doubt and fear. The Bible says,

> *What good is it, my brothers, if a man claims to have faith but has no deeds? Can such faith save him? Suppose a brother or sister is without clothes and daily food. If one of you says to him, "Go, I wish you well; keep warm and well fed," but does nothing about his physical needs, what good is it? In the same way, faith by itself, if it is not accompanied by action, is dead* (James 2:14-17).

Roger Bannister is a name many will remember. When the world, doctors and science said no one could run a one-mile race in less than four minutes, Roger Bannister asked himself, "How can it be done?" This was a man who had already lost a race in the Olympics. Yet he did not allow his failure to stop him. Indeed, he used his failure to coach him into a new level of excellence. Failure was his stepping stone to a success that broke a new world record. He was a risk-taker.

How do you handle failure? Will you allow past blunders to hinder present blessings? Roger Bannister didn't. He made up his mind that he would defy man's limitation and do what was declared impossible.

Scientists had declared that the molecular structure of the human body made it impossible for anyone to run a one-mile race in less than four minutes. That was a present reality. Roger Bannister, however, stepped into another reality and broke the current world record. He did it in 3 minutes 59.4 seconds, pacing himself with the help of a team of timers at the end of each lap. His act of faith and the use of his brain made him win with more than just muscular strength.

Once the record was broken, many slipstreamed behind him and broke his record. Records are being broken every day by risk-takers. Why? Because people with faith still dare to believe, work hard and exercise the greatness of God that is within.

In the New Testament book of James, he talks about showing faith by your deeds. Faith without action is dead (James 2:26). Because we believe, we "do" something about what we believe. Moses' step of faith into the Red Sea created a ripple that turned into a tsunami that divided it for millions to go through into safety (Exodus 15). As a risk-taker your step of faith will create a ripple that God will turn into a tsunami to break all barriers to your success. The supernatural is waiting on your natural choices and step of faith.

FAITH WITHOUT ACTION DIES

Faith and action go hand in hand. The Bible says *"As the body without the spirit is dead, so faith without deeds is dead"* (James 2:26). In other words, when faith comes to you even as you read this book, if you do not act on your faith it will eventually die. Death is the separation of the human spirit from its body. Death of faith comes when a dream is devoid of action.

Faith is an attitude. Attitude is action. It is a choice that becomes a personality. A positive attitude creates the strength to actually do something with your faith.

Planning is faith in action. Make plans to achieve your dreams. Your planning is the first step that will create a ripple effect. Planning and long-term thinking make best friends. It is said, "If you fail to plan, you plan to fail."

According to Murray, you get God's attention and support with your faith-based commitment to your dreams. Your commitment to your desire releases tangible and intangible things to support your decision for action. While you may have obstacles along the way to test the authenticity of your commitment, the power of your faith will keep you going once you step out of the boat!

SACRIFICIAL FAITH

Finally, you must be willing to make sacrifices for what you believe in. Sacrifice means to deny yourself for a greater purpose. Parents continually sacrifice for their children. The family is based on sacrificial giving and forgiving. No sacrifice is without a greater reward than what was given up.

In the movie *John Q*, we see the story of a father, played by Denzel Washington, who was willing to sacrifice whatever it took to save the life of his only son, Michael. This ordinary man, John Q. Archibald, whose life revolved around his family, became a hero as in desperation when his son became seriously ill and needed an emergency heart transplant he held hostages in a hospital, demanding a heart for his son. He was poor and could not afford to pay for the services to save his son's life. He was willing to die to give his own heart to save his son's life. His sacrificial faith moved him to desperate actions. He was a risk-taker. His son did get a heart transplant and his life was spared because of a father who loved enough to sacrifice his own life for his son.

Dr. Martin Luther King Jr. knew that his life was on the line when he vocalized his dreams of seeing a united world despite racial differences. Even years after his death, his dreams are being realized every day around the world.

Bill Gates sacrificed his pre-law degree to pursue his computer technology interests. Today he is one of the world's richest billionaires. Rosa Parks, a woman from the Civil Rights era, sacrificed her physical freedom for freedom of equality when she was arrested for refusing to give up her bus seat because she was black.

You cannot get something for nothing. *"A man reaps what he sows"* (Galatians 6:7) applies to every arena of our lives. If you sow seeds of faith, persistence, and patience in all areas of your life, you will in turn reap the rewards of that sowing.

Athletes sacrifice much. For four years they discipline themselves, sacrificing their time and social life in order to obtain a greater reward. To win an Olympic medal is their goal. It is an attainable goal. They visualize themselves one day standing in the centre of the stadium with that medallion draped around their necks and the entire audience standing in allegiance to their country's national anthem. They are willing to sacrifice food, fun, and social events to get to their prize.

God sacrificed His Son, Jesus Christ, to die on the cross for the sins of the world. Love sacrifices. Faith demands sacrifice.

As you embrace the great walk of faith, daily remind yourself:

- Faith works.
- Planning and faith go hand in hand.
- Walk in the spirit or attitude of faith.
- Anything worth believing for is worth sacrificing for.
- By faith, you can create your world using *The Ultimate Secret*.

Part Two

POWER TO ASK

"Ask and it will be given to you; seek and you will find; knock and the door will be opened to you."

(Matthew 7:7)

Six

JUST ASK

Have you ever been sitting in a crowded class or seminar where there was a forum for questions and answers? Did you note how many people asked questions and how many remained silent? It is not that the silent people had no question, but they were either afraid to speak or chose not exert the effort to receive the information.

THE SECOND PRINCIPLE TO THE ULTIMATE SECRET—THE POWER TO ASK

A Danish proverb states "He who is afraid of asking is ashamed of learning." It takes humility to ask. It takes humility to pray. Prayer means admitting that you cannot do it all on your own, that you do not have everything figured out and that you need God. Jesus said, *"Ask and it will be given to you"* (Matthew 7:7). In James 4:2 we are told, *"You do not have, because you do not ask God."*

Opening your heart before God, being honest and upfront with Him, pleases God, as your transparency is a sign of your humility and faith. The word *prayer* means communion and conversation with God. It means to ask for your desire or ask as you seek the desires of God. Prayer is oftentimes asking God for what He has already promised, based on His Word. God is waiting for you to ask so that He can answer and give you His desires for you. God wants to bless, protect and provide for you. As your Heavenly Father, God is committed to you. When you pray, you strengthen your relationship with God.

The Power to Ask is a wonderful privilege. Jesus challenged His disciples: *"Therefore I tell you, whatever you ask for in prayer, believe that you have received it, and it will be yours"* (Mark 11:24). The Creator of life and the universe has given us the opportunity to ask Him for whatever, whenever. This is like receiving a signed blank cheque from a billionaire who gives you the privilege to purchase whatever you want whenever with His guaranteed endorsement. The greatness of the privilege, however, is that a billionaire is still limited. God is called The Most High. He has unlimited resources. What is not He can create. What is created He can destroy. He is not just your Provider but He is Creator.

God works *for* you when you pray. God works *with* you when you act. God has given you power and dominion to rule your world. He gave us the earth, but we created our world. We have a free will to choose our path. So when we pray, we give God permission to intervene in our world and to help us to create His design and destiny for our lives. Our asking releases His will for our lives. For instance, God wants to give us wisdom, but He says, *"If any of you lacks wisdom, he should ask God, who gives generously to all without finding fault, and it will be given to him"* (James 1:5).

God wants you to love Him, share your life with Him and pray to Him. This is called relating and strengthening your relationship with God. He wants to heal you, but He says,

> *Is any one of you sick? He should call the elders of the church to pray over him and anoint him with oil in the name of the Lord. And the prayer offered in faith will make the sick person well; the Lord will raise him up. If he has sinned, he will be forgiven* (James 5:14-15).

God will not violate your will. Your choice is to ask Him for your desires. He is sovereign, mighty and powerful, but He is also merciful, loving and compassionate and requires relationship. He will not force His will and purpose in your life regardless of how beautiful His design is for you. Therefore it is up to you to ask Him for your desires. The Bible further states *"For everyone to whom much is given, from him much will be required"* (Luke 12:48, NKJV). You will be responsible for developing your gifts and talents, for having the wisdom to grow in financial strength and to make good use of any territory (land or sphere of influence) given to you. You are powerfully made in the image of God with creative ability and likeness to His nature. You have the spiritual DNA of God.

Asking Is Humility

As I stated before, prayer is a sign of humility. It is recognition that we need to connect, relate and at times depend on God. When we ask of God, we glorify Him. God is not burdened with our requests. He wants to hear from us. Jesus said, *"Come to me, all you who are weary and burdened, and I will give you rest"* (Matthew 11:28). We are also told, *"Cast all your anxiety on him because he cares for you"* (1 Peter 5:7).

Asking Helps Us to Define Our Desires

If you have never thought about what you want in life and suddenly you bump into a billionaire and he says, "I am going to invest money in some of your desires. What do you want to do?" what would you to tell him? When you are given the opportunity to ask God for anything that you want or dream of having, you are challenged to put definition to your vision and desires. Any confusion that you may have fought will banish as you think and vocalize your thoughts. Even if you do not know what you want but ask God to show you what you *should* want or need, you will obtain an inner peace because you have laid your own concerns on someone greater than yourself.

I love communicating with God, because He is not only my Saviour but also my guide and heavenly Father. It is a great privilege to commune with Him! I do not have to ask for any specific thing every time I commune with Him. I can just talk to Him about my day, or about a project I'm working on, or about something I have learned.

It is wonderful to know that God looks for ways to bless us. God sometimes asks, "What can I do for you?" In fact, there was a young man who was asked that by God. In 2 Chronicles 1, we read the story of Solomon, who was a young man when he became king, succeeding his father King David. He established himself over his kingdom by listening to the wise counsellors that God had connected to him. His humility made him become a great leader. He was strong in making decisions followed by timely actions. His heart was nurtured by great mentors and God, to whom he was divinely connected in submission, reverence and communion.

God appeared to Solomon in a dream one night and said to him, *"Ask for whatever you want me to give you"* (1 Kings 3:5). Wow! What an opportunity to ask for whatever from God who has unlimited resources. Solomon could have asked for more power, riches, the head of his enemies and a larger palace. Instead, he asked God for His wisdom and knowledge to govern His great people. Look at the interchange between God and Solomon. Note God's response.

> *"Give me wisdom and knowledge, that I may lead this people, for who is able to govern this great people of yours?" God said to Solomon, "Since this is your heart's desire and you have not asked for wealth, riches or honor, nor for the death of your enemies, and since you have not asked for a long life but for wisdom and knowledge to govern my people over whom I have made you king, therefore wisdom and knowledge will be given you. And I will also give you wealth, riches and honor, such as no king who was before you ever had and none after you will have"* (2 Chronicles 1:10-12).

God is not only able to take care of your needs, but He will always give you more than you ask for. As Ephesians 3:20 says, *"Now to him who is able to do immeasurably more than all we ask or imagine, according to his power that is at work within us."*

"If you believe, you will receive whatever you ask for in prayer" (Matthew 21:22).

ASK THE RIGHT PERSON

Prayer engages spiritual power. It is connecting to a person or personality in the spiritual realm. Therefore, you must make sure you are connecting to the right *person* and spiritual source. When you turn on your radio, you decide whether you want FM or AM. In the same way, you must know to whom you are praying. Remember, prayer is not communication with a person but with a *personality.*

Earlier we discussed the character and nature of God. Jesus in John 16:23 tells us how to target our prayer life: *"In that day you will no longer ask me anything. I tell you the truth, my Father will give you whatever you ask in my name."* Jesus' mission on earth was to restore relationship between God and man and to teach us to relate to Him as our heavenly Father. As He was about to leave this earth, his goal was to fulfill that mission, beginning with His disciples. Jesus, as the Son of God, related to Him as Father. The Father called Him *"my beloved Son"* (Matthew 3:17; 17:5, KJV). This beautiful relationship is now ours as we become children of God.

To strengthen our asking He encourages us to ask God as our Father and to do so in His name. Look at the promise that comes with praying in Jesus' name. *"My Father will give you whatever you ask in my name"* (John 16:23). That means we can know in advance that we have what we ask of God because we ask it in the name of his Son, Jesus Christ.

Jesus goes on to say, *"Until now you have not asked for anything in my name. Ask and you will receive, and your joy will be complete"*

(John 16:24). God wants you to have significance. He wants you to have joy, and not just joy but *complete* joy. He really wants nothing missing, nothing broken and full joy in your life. Those are not my words but the words of Jesus Christ. Jesus wants us to ask God in prayer. When you ask, you are to believe that you receive whatever you ask for in prayer, and it will be yours (Mark 11:24).

I am reminded about George Washington Carver being born in slavery. In addition, he was a sick child. He had some physical ailments. Because of this, he was not sent out to work on the farm like the other children but was kept in the kitchen. It was there that the best in Carver was revealed as he worked with food and created recipes.

He later became an agricultural chemist, a scientist. It is said that one day he was praying (he understood the principle of asking God in prayer). He said, "Mr. Creator, show me the secrets of your universe." This is a great question. God answered this young man and said, "You want to know the secrets of my universe, but let's just start right now with a simple process because you are not big enough to know the secrets of my universe. I will show you the secret of a peanut."

I pause here to note that one of the keys in moving from desolation to your destiny is for God to give you *revelation*. God's answers at times will come as guidance and direction.

Your destiny includes coaching. In humility, Carver obeyed God and began to take a little seed of a peanut apart in the little kitchen that he had. He did not have a fancy studio and lab; he decided to start with what he had and to put his faith to action. George Washington Carver discovered that there are 700 elements in the peanut. God continued the coaching and told him to rearrange the elements to create different products. Just as hydrogen and oxygen, two separate gases, when combined make water, God revealed to Carver the diversifications and combinations of the elements of the peanut. He was able to create peanut butter, soap, oil, cosmetics, etc. You now have peanut butter because of George Carver. Ask God for a revelation of your destiny. God speaks, guides and coaches those who come to Him in humility and confidence to ask Him for whatever, whenever.

GOD IS WAITING TO ANSWER YOU

God wants to answer you. But you have to ask. He wants to give you fresh revelation, but you have to seek Him. Psalm 32:8 says, *"I will instruct you and teach you in the way you should go; I will counsel you and watch over you."*

Jeremiah 33:3 also encourages us, with *"Call to me and I will answer you and tell you great and unsearchable things you do not know."* Now you know that God is waiting to hear from you. Just ask.

Seven

BE SPECIFIC

On many occasions when Jesus was approached by someone for a miracle, He would ask them direct questions to expose the content of their hearts. He listened for specifics, faith, confidence and tenacity.

God encourages over and over in His word to ask for whatever, whenever:

> *"I will do whatever you ask in my name, so that the Son may bring glory to the Father. You may ask me for anything in my name, and I will do it"* (John 14:13-14).

> *"If you remain in me and my words remain in you, ask whatever you wish, and it will be given you"* (John 15:7).

> *"In that day you will no longer ask me anything. I tell you the truth, my Father will give you whatever you ask in my name. Until now you have not asked for anything in my name. Ask and you will receive, and your joy will be complete"* (John 16:23-24).

> *"This is the confidence we have in approaching God: that if we ask anything according to his will, he hears us. And if we know that he hears us—whatever we ask—we know that we have what we asked of him"* (1 John 5:14-15).

"Until now you have not asked for anything in my name. Ask and you will receive, and your joy will be complete" (John 16:24).

Jesus reveals our heavenly Father's heart and open invitation for us to ask Him whatever, whenever.

"Ask and it will be given to you; seek and you will find; knock and the door will be opened to you. For everyone who asks receives; he who seeks finds; and to him who knocks, the door will be opened. Which of you, if his son asks for bread, will give him a stone? Or if he asks for a fish, will give him a snake? If you, then, though you are evil, know how to give good gifts to your children, how much more will your Father in heaven give good gifts to those who ask him!" (Matthew 7:7-11).

We are encouraged not only to ask God for our desires but also to be specific with our asking, for we will receive specifically what we ask for. That is very specific and involves activating our thought and planning process to a higher level before asking.

The Bible tells the story in John chapter 5 of Jesus and His disciples going to Jerusalem for a feast. The feasts and festivals were highlights and pilgrimages to the city several times a year. Jerusalem was a walled city with several towers and gates. In the northeastern part of Jerusalem, near the Sheep Gate, was a natural spring called Bethesda that was a source of attraction for its earliest occupants. It was believed that at certain times of the year an angel would come and release healing virtue in the pool. Five colonnades were constructed to accommodate the crowd, and the site became known as the Pool at Bethesda. A great number of sick people would line up for days wanting to go into the pool for healing and miracles at the time when *"an angel went down...and stirred up the water"* (v. 4, NKJV).

As Jesus came near to the region of the pool, He saw a man lying there, and He inquired about him. He learned that the man had been crippled for thirty-eight years. Jesus was moved with compassion, as He often was when He saw the suffering of people, whether it was physical, emotional or spiritual suffering. The Bible says,

> *Jesus went throughout Galilee, teaching in their synagogues, preaching the good news of the kingdom, and healing every disease and sickness among the people. News about him spread all over Syria, and people brought to him all who were ill with various diseases, those suffering severe pain, the demon-possessed, those having seizures, and the paralyzed, and he healed them. Large crowds from Galilee, the Decapolis, Jerusalem, Judea and the region across the Jordan followed him* (Matthew 4:23-25)

Jesus approached the man and asked him, *"Do you want to get well?"* (John 5:6). This was a specific question that required a specific answer. As a matter of fact, only a "yes" would have been perfect. The crippled man, however, missed his "cue" and ignored the "clues." Being sensitive to "cues" and "clues" is very important, as ignoring them can result in unnecessary and greater complications.

A clue is a "sound bite" from someone that puts you in an "Aha moment," as unknown to them they have revealed their heart, intention and meditation. A clue brings awareness and is a sign that action might be needed. A clue can come from someone's behaviour, what they say or don't say or what they do or don't do. Our weather report is based on understanding clues and making predictions.

A clue should motivate you to action, which is your cue. In live theatre when the curtain opens and the lights are on, it means it is time for action. This is not a rehearsal; this is the moment— you are on! You cannot afford to miss your cue.

Sometimes life throws us circumstances that are not rehearsals. Things are set in motion waiting for your turn. If you miss your turn or your cue, it could trigger severe consequences. Understanding clues and cues are very important in all relationships. Imagine if parents could pick up clues when a child becomes distressed because of negative peer pressure and is about to do something "just to fit in" that could result in expulsion from school or involvement with the law. On many occasions it is just being at the wrong place at the wrong time, and a child can miss the clue that spells *danger.*

As we gain sensitivity in this area, it will eliminate some of the negative surprises in business, family, health and in relationships. Our physical body gives us "clues" about health issues that require "cues" for correction.

The man at Bethesda who had been crippled for thirty-eight years had no clue that he was approached by Jesus, the Christ, with the anointing to heal him. Instead of a specific answer to the question *"Do you want to get well?"* he began to complain. *"'Sir,' the invalid replied, 'I have no one to help me into the pool when the water is stirred. While I am trying to get in, someone else goes down ahead of me"* (John 5:7). This was a clue to Jesus that this man's long-term condition of paralysis had negatively affected his heart. He was ready to blame others, ready to obtain pity, ready to speak of his condition, but not ready for intervention. His language was from an attitude of hopelessness and not faith.

Remember that hope is the mother of faith. Although it is difficult when trials are long-term, you have the choice to keep your heart whole and your faith alive. You have the inner power of choice and will, and with God's help your heart will be strengthened and preserved.

Notice this man's answer to the simple question "Do you want to get well?"

1. *"I have no one to help me."* Wow! He missed a big clue. Jesus Christ the Healer was standing right beside him—not just a helper but the Healer. His cue should have been a "yes!"

2. *"While I am trying to get in, someone else goes down ahead of me."*

Meaning, others are selfish; it not my fault; I am just unlucky; poor me. He missed another big clue. The bells in his mind were silent. A "ding dong" should have gone off as He looked into the eyes of Jesus, the Saviour, Helper, Healer. Even Bartimaeus, a blind man who was sitting begging on the side of the road at Jericho, had the *insight* to call out to Jesus when he heard that He was passing by (Mark 10:46-47). That man was healed, for he specifically asked for his sight to be restored. This man, however, was not only crippled in his body but also in his heart. His long-term suffering had released poison to his soul that had destroyed his hope.

Jesus, in mercy and loving kindness, ignored the man's complaints and ignorance of who He was and what He could do. *"Then Jesus said to him, 'Get up! Pick up your mat and walk.' At once the man was cured; he picked up his mat and walked"* (John 5:8-9). God looks for opportunities to help the helpless.

David wrote a psalm of love and gratefulness describing the love and compassion of God:

> *Praise the LORD, O my soul, and forget not all his bene-fits—who forgives all your sins and heals all your diseases, who redeems your life from the pit and crowns you with love and compassion, who satisfies your desires with good things so that your youth is renewed like the eagle's* (Psalm 103:2-5).

Just ask, but be specific. God is working for you. His great power is ready to be released to you if only you would ask.

A desperate father dared to ask Jesus for the healing of his daughter.

> *When Jesus had again crossed over by boat to the other side of the lake, a large crowd gathered around him while he was by the lake. Then one of the synagogue rulers, named Jairus, came there. Seeing Jesus, he fell at his feet and pleaded earnestly with him, "My little daughter is dying. Please come and put your hands on her so that she will be healed and live." So Jesus went with him* (Mark 5:21-24).

This proves that in a world of over six billion people, God is never too busy to hear your cry or listen to your question. Jesus changed His focus and direction in response to the "ask" of the desperate father. He went to the home of Jairus and took his daughter by the hand and released healing power into her weakened body. *"Immediately the girl stood up and walked around (she was twelve years old). At this they were completely astonished"* (Mark 5:42).

You can ask God specifically for your needs and for the needs of others. Your asking releases His divine power to create, heal, bless, provide and protect you and those whom you ask for.

ASKING AMISS

The word *amiss* means "away from the correct or expected course; to do something in an improper manner or to imperfectly function." The King James version says, *"Ye ask, and receive not, because ye ask amiss, that ye may consume it upon your lusts"* (James 4:2-3). The New International Version puts it this way: *"You do not have, because you do not ask God. When you ask, you do not receive, because you ask with wrong motives, that you may spend what you get on your pleasures."*

God will give you the desires of your heart as you keep your motives pure and pray according to His will. If your motive is greed or to hurt others, you are asking amiss. Desiring a good husband or wife is a good thing. But wanting *someone else's* good husband or wife is not. That is asking amiss. You are communicating your desires to God, which is good, but you are praying for the wrong thing and with the wrong motives.

If you want to make sure that you are not asking amiss or asking with the wrong motives, you must first of all check your desires. These are questions that could help to purify desires when you are unsure:

• What is my motive?
• Will this answer hurt anyone?

- Will my answer benefit others?
- Will my answer create unity or disunity?
- Is my desire against the Word of God?
- Is my desire pleasing to God?

Truthful and upright answers to those questions will help to guide you in ensuring that you are praying for the right thing, with the right motives, and that you will do the right thing with what you receive when you receive it.

Praying God's will automatically get God's attention. First John 5:14-15 says, *"This is the confidence we have in approaching God: that if we ask anything according to his will, he hears us. And if we know that he hears us—whatever we ask—we know that we have what we asked of him."*

God has given us His Word that contains His will for our lives, for our families, for our purpose in life and for our world. Once we know His will, we can pray or ask with confidence, knowing that we will receive the answers to our prayer. Here is a list of things that God declares in His Word as His will for you:

- His peace
- Your personal salvation and relationship with Him
- His forgiveness
- Good health
- Blessings on you and your family
- Prosperity
- Protection
- Guidance
- Strength
- Success in your calling and career
- Knowing His voice
- Generational blessings

Then there are items where we must seek God's specific will for us, such as:

- Job or career
- Spouse
- College or university
- Church to attend
- Making decisions

The first category is God's will for us based on His promises to us in His Word. However, regarding the second category, we must be willing to listen and be guided for specifics to be revealed in those areas. If we ask God's guidance in buying a house, we might not hear a clear voice saying, "Buy this one." Sometimes God leads us through circumstances and closed or opened doors. He may speak through others and sometimes guides us on the inside through intuition, a sense of direction and a feeling of peace or lack of peace.

As you continue in the journey of prayer you will sense His leading more and more and become more confident in His guidance.

PAT'S POINTS

- Have faith in God.
- Relate to God as your Father.
- Get to know His Word and promises.
- Pray the promises of God.
- Ask God for whatever, whenever.
- Be tenacious.
- Be expectant.
- Believe that you have received.
- Just ask.
- Be specific.
- Give thanks with a grateful heart.

Eight

THE ASKING TEMPLATE OF JESUS

We teach our children the protocol for asking using the "magic word," "please." We teach the attitude for asking and the reciprocal "Thank you." Jesus taught us how to pray, how to approach our Heavenly Father with the right protocol and how to ask to receive.

Jesus taught us how to pray in Matthew 6:9-13:

"This, then, is how you should pray: 'Our Father in heaven, hallowed be your name, your kingdom come, your will be done on earth as it is in heaven. Give us today our daily bread. Forgive us our debts, as we also have forgiven our debtors. And lead us not into temptation, but deliver us from the evil one.'"

OUR FATHER IN HEAVEN

When addressing God, address Him as Father. Establish your covenant relationship with God as your Father. There are many names of God recorded in the Bible. He is referred to as the Ancient of Days (Daniel 7:9,13,22) and the righteous Judge (Psalm 7:11; 2 Timothy 4:8). Jesus is saying, when you come to God, come not as one coming to only a judge but to your daddy.

In the atmosphere of a court, a judge can be very intimidating. However, if that powerful judge is also your daddy, then you feel free to run and ask him to fix your bicycle when he comes home. A prime minister or president is a powerful person in the seat of government, but when that person gets home to his covenant family, the role and expectations are different. His favour and grace towards his family are different from his grace towards the citizens in his country.

While respecting the presence of God and acknowledge His power, you must approach Him as your loving Father who is committed to our care, provision and protection. As your Heavenly Father, He desires communion, fellowship and the opportunity to share His heart and purpose for you and our world. As a good Father, He will redeem you out of trouble and give you daily mercy and grace.

Psalm 68:5 says, *"A father to the fatherless, a defender of widows, is God in his holy dwelling."* Psalm 89:26 says, *"He will call out to me, 'You are my Father, my God, the Rock my Savior.'"* Psalm 103:13 says, *"As a father has compassion on his children, so the LORD has compassion on those who fear him."* God's words and thoughts toward you are filled with compassion and mercy. God is your Heavenly Father.

Jesus then goes on to the second statement in the prayer:

HALLOWED BE YOUR NAME

We must revere and respect the name of the Lord. That is why the Bible says we should not use the Lord's name in vain (Deuteronomy 5:11, NKJV). Psalm 20:7 says, *"Some trust in chariots and some in horses, but we trust in the name of the LORD our God."* Proverbs 18:10 says, *"The name of the LORD is a strong tower; the righteous run to it and are safe."* When you are in a crisis, run to the Name.

The Bible has compound names of God. This means that God often combines His Name with the action that He is willing to perform. For example His Name is *Jehovah* (God) and when combined with *Jireh* (Provider) *Jehovah Jireh* means "The Lord

God Your Provider." As you learn these names, they will help you in praying specifically to release a specific action according to your need.

Here are some names of God that will specifically manifest according to your need:

Jehovah Rophe: The Lord is my Healer.
Jehovah Jireh: The Lord is my Provider.
Jehovah Nissi: The Lord is my Banner, the God who cheers me on to victory.
Jehovah Rohi: The Lord is my Shepherd, the One who leads and guides me.
Jehovah Shalom: The Lord is my Peace and my Prosperity.
Jehovah Shammah: The Lord's Presence is always with me; I am never alone.
Jehovah Tsidkenu: The Lord is my Righteousness; I am forgiven.

When you exalt His Name He will manifest the Name you exalt and work on your behalf.

Worship and thanksgiving is therefore the protocol for entering the presence of His Holiness. You must revere, exalt, respect and worship His Holy Name. As you worship His Holy Name, acknowledge His power, His love and His presence. Begin and end your prayer with worship and thanksgiving. To end with thanksgiving is your assurance of faith that you have received what you have asked for.

Then Jesus goes on to say to pray,

YOUR KINGDOM COME, YOUR WILL BE DONE, ON EARTH AS IT IS IN HEAVEN

Jesus spoke frequently about the kingdom of God. Matthew 4:23 says, *"Jesus went throughout Galilee, teaching in their synagogues, preaching the good news of the kingdom."* A kingdom is a system governed by a king where the king rules over a territory (land, systems, institutions and people). In earthly kingdoms, there are distinct elements, such as a king or queen; a specific territory of influence (nation); laws and citizens of the kingdom. Jesus came to establish His Kingdom on earth. His Kingdom is spiritual and not natural. He is the King and Ruler of His Kingdom. Those who believe in Him enter His Kingdom and become members of His Royal Family. Although He is Creator of the earth, the territory that He controls in our world is the territory that mankind submits to His rulership. With the power of choice, you can choose the kingdom that rules and the laws that you live by.

The Bible refers to three kingdoms: the kingdom of Satan (who rules with evil), the kingdom of mankind (government leaders) and the kingdom of God (God is King and all who believes in Him are a part of His Kingdom).

The Kingdom of God, like every kingdom, has laws or a constitution. In His Kingdom, our laws or constitution is the Bible, containing His Word, will and wisdom. God has a Kingdom purpose for every person in the earth. He has a Kingdom purpose for our family, our career or business and our spiritual life. Regardless of the path in life that we choose—our career—creation of wealth is wrapped up in our "calling." You are called of God for significance in this world. The Bible says, *"For we are God's workmanship, created in Christ Jesus to do good works, which God prepared in advance for us to do"* (Ephesians 2:10). Everything about you is important to Him. Your life on earth is important to Him, as you are His representative. He lives in you and can flow through you to influence your world with His goodness and godliness.

Jesus teaches us to pray with His Kingdom as the first priority. Pray *"your kingdom come, your will be done on earth as it is in heaven"* (Matthew 6:10). Here He states that God has a divine plan for our lives, a blueprint that we must pray into manifestation. This is submission to the King, believing that His Will is the ultimate plan with a divine purpose that might not yet be revealed. His Kingdom purpose for you, your family and all areas of your life is the optimum prosperity with guaranteed success. You are a member of God's royal family, in His Kingdom, with the King as your Heavenly Father. Your benefits in His Kingdom include peace, good health, prosperity, love, joy and righteousness as you enjoy a full Kingdom life.

When you pray this prayer, you are saying over and over again, "Lord, you are King in my life. I submit to your will and your purpose. I trust you as my King who knows all things and sees all things, including the future that I cannot see. I am safe and secure in your Kingdom and my trust is in You."

Jesus goes on to say to pray,

GIVE US TODAY OUR DAILY BREAD

Do not be afraid to *ask* God for the desires of your heart. Ask. Here Jesus encourages you to nurture your relationship with your Heavenly Father with daily communion and daily asking for provision, protection and direction.

God wants you to take one day at a time with a conscious submission of that day into His care and keeping. Although you may have long-term plans, you must enjoy each day and live it to the fullest without worry about tomorrow. In fact, He urges us to *"not worry about tomorrow, for tomorrow will worry about itself. Each day has enough trouble of its own"* (Matthew 6:34). *Daily bread* means daily provision!

Worry erodes faith. We read, *"And my God will meet all your needs according to his glorious riches in Christ Jesus"* (Philippians 4:19). God's glorious riches cannot be counted. So consider that whenever you think about your needs. He is supplying out of His own storehouse! Ask.

Jesus says to pray:

FORGIVE US OUR DEBTS...

Ask for forgiveness. It is not *if* we ever need forgiveness but *when.* Jesus frees us to come daily to God, acknowledging our imperfections, and ask for His forgiveness. This is a relief. God knows that none of us are perfect. He knows that mistakes and disappointments are human traits. You love your children and are committed to them for life. So is God committed to you forever. He loves you and will forgive all your sins as you ask for forgiveness. God is not waiting to condemn you. The Word of God is clear on that:

> *"For God so loved the world that he gave his one and only Son, that whoever believes in him shall not perish but have eternal life. For God did not send his Son into the world to condemn the world, but to save the world through him"* (John 3:16-17).

God will forgive us whenever we ask for His forgiveness.

As We Also Have Forgiven Our Debtors

Forgiving others frees your soul and frees God to forgive you also. The Bible says, *"Blessed are the merciful, for they will be shown mercy* (Matthew 5:7). Forgiveness is a choice and not a feeling. Harbouring grudges, bitterness, malice and hatred in the heart creates poison in the soul. Hurts and disappointments come in all relationships. As human beings we disappoint each other. Forgiveness promotes the health and well-being of the soul. The Bible encourages us to *"Get rid of all bitterness, rage and anger, brawling and slander, along with every form of malice. Be kind and compassionate to one another, forgiving each other, just as in Christ God forgave you"* (Ephesians 4:31-32).

Margaret Davidson shares her story of repeated sexual abuse by her older brother and how God led her to the journey of forgiveness and complete freedom. By forgiving her brother she freed herself and became opened to the grace of God to travel and set other women free. In the Kingdom of this world people can choose evil. Evil influences hearts and creates evil hearts. Victims, however, can free themselves by the power of forgiveness.

You have the power to free yourself from unhealthy soul ties by forgiving those who have wronged you in the past. When you are set free you will soar to new heights of peace and well-being. True freedom is within. Forgiveness is powerful to break the chains and liberate the soul. It is the key to wholeness.

And Lead Us Not into Temptation, but Deliver Us from the Evil One

Here God reveals more of the evil kingdom of Satan. Even as God is described by many names, so is Satan. He is called the Evil One, the Devil, a liar, a murderer, a deceiver, a slanderer, a thief and a destroyer. When we pray *"Lead us not into temptation,"* we are asking for God's guidance in all our decisions. We are asking God to provide warnings and a way of escape even as He empowers us to resist the temptation. The temptation could be a trap in a business deal, a fatal attraction or to lash out in anger and say words that can never be taken back.

God has promised to protect you so that, whatever temptation you may face, He will empower you to successfully resist it. If you fall into a trap, look for the way of escape that God will provide. First Corinthians 10:13 says, *"No temptation has seized you except what is common to man* [yes, that means someone's been there before]. *And God is faithful; he will not let you be tempted beyond what you can bear. But when you are tempted, he will also provide a way out so that you can stand up under it."* In essence, when Jesus said *"lead us not into temptation, but deliver us from the evil one,'* He was acknowledging that temptation is there, that's a reality, but with His help, we will walk in wisdom and discretion and keep in right standing with God.

When we pray *"deliver us from the evil one,"* we are asking God to protect us from all the attacks of evil. Jesus told us the agenda of Satan: *"The thief comes only to steal and kill and destroy; I have come that they may have life, and have it to the full"* (John 10:10). Satan will try to steal, kill and destroy our relationships, our health, our finances, our families and anything that is not covered by the power of God or submitted to His Kingdom.

Jesus Christ has a vendetta against evil and the evil one, as stated: *"The reason the Son of God appeared was to destroy the devil's work"* (1 John 3:8). Your *"ask"* will activate the power of God to destroy the devil's work in your life and in all that concerns you.

So far, we have studied two keys of *The Ultimate Secret:* faith and ask. Have *faith* in God, and *ask* God for the desires of your heart.

PAT'S POINTS

- Jesus gave us a template for effective asking.
- God is waiting for your "ask."
- Begin your *"ask"* with worship.
- Ask daily for forgiveness, provision, protection.
- Asking must not be selfish.
- Ask with His will in mind.
- Ask in faith.
- Be specific when you ask.
- End your asking with thanksgiving and praise.

Part Three

POWER TO BELIEVE

*"You can have anything you want if you will give
up the belief that you can't have it."*

Dr. Robert Anthony

Nine

METHOD OF BELIEVING

The third key of The Ultimate Secret is the Power to Believe.

You are what you believe. So whatever you believe, you conceive in the womb of your heart and become or create.

A *belief system* is a way of thinking, a mental state in which we hold certain propositions or premises to be true. According to Wikipedia, belief is divided into *core beliefs* (those that you actively think about, such as a way of religion, or culture) and *dispositional beliefs* (beliefs you hold on to but never really think about). You might hold on to a belief given to you by your parents without every thinking it through yourself.

Belief is a state of mind. Beliefs are ideologies, concepts—a person can agree or disagree with them. Beliefs are not necessarily the truth. They are very subjective and therefore relative to the truth. Beliefs can cause people to debate with one another for hours about something never proven to be either true or false. Beliefs shape our faith and create our attitude. It is the framework of thoughts and ideas whereby individuals interpret what they hear, the world, people and relationships.

Our belief is often shaped by systems that we know to be true. For instance, we believe that 1+5 = 6. We believe this because we were taught the value of 1 and 5 and that if we add those two together, their values will amount to the value of 6. This is because we were inculcated with a certain belief system in numbering. As children, we were taught to believe and live by this numbering system. Our world economy is based on this numbering system.

The difference between a belief and faith is that a belief is mental and is influenced by the external, while faith is spiritual and determined by choice. Belief is supported by the physical senses (hearing, touching, tasting, smelling, feeling); faith on the other hand does not need proof to hold on to what it believes. Further, faith affirms that what we believe is *real*, even if only to us. This gives us a clearer understanding of why the Bible says in Hebrews 11:1, "*Faith is the substance of things hoped for, the evidence of things not seen*" (NKJV).

For the purpose of this chapter, we will focus on *dispositional beliefs*. These are systems that we subconsciously ascribe to.

Your Beliefs Affect Every Area of Your Life

The story is told of a large mountainside where an eagle's nest rested. Inside were four large eagle eggs. One day an earthquake rocked the mountain, causing one of the eggs to roll down to a chicken farm located in the valley below. The chickens knew that they must protect and care for the eagle's egg, so an old hen nurtured and raise the large egg.

The egg hatched, and a beautiful eagle was born. However, the eagle was raised to be a chicken. He ate with chickens. He flocked with chickens. He moved like a chicken. As a result, the eagle believed that he was nothing more than a chicken. He loved his home and family, but his spirit cried out for more. While out with the chickens on the farm one day, the eagle looked up and noticed a group of mighty eagles soaring in the skies. "Oh," the eagle cried, "I wish I could soar like those birds."

The chickens rolled over with laughter. "You cannot soar with those birds. You are a chicken, and chickens do not soar." The eagle continued staring at his real family soaring through the skies, wishing he could be with them. Each time the eagle would let his dreams be known, he was told it couldn't be done.

Because of this, he eventually gave up on his dreams and continued to live his life like a chicken. After a long life as a chicken, the eagle passed away.

Your belief system shapes how you live your life, how you interact with others, how you interact with yourself, how you see yourself and what you dare to dream. Picture a lion staring into a mirror and seeing the reflection of a cat and at the top of this image are the words "What matters most is how you see yourself."

The eagle saw himself as a chicken. He *believed* he was a chicken, not only because of what he was told, but also because of how he was brought up. He never lived the life of an eagle, even though every fibre of his being was that of an eagle. His mentality was stronger than his physical nature. He could not fly like an eagle, because someone told him he could not fly like an eagle. He could not fly like an eagle, because he *believed* exactly what he was told. For that reason, he was forever affected by his beliefs. What you believe, you become.

Whether you realize it or not, your pattern of thinking influences every area of your life. The Bible puts it this way: *"As [a man] thinks in his heart, so is he"* (Proverbs 23:7, NKJV). Your eating habits, your dress code, the way you speak, the goals you try to obtain and the ones you're afraid to attain, the friends you have, the church you attend and where and how you spend your money are oftentimes an indication of your beliefs, conscious and subconscious.

We often hear about poor people winning the lottery and then after a few months, or even two years, they are back to being poor. No one robbed them and no one went into their bank accounts and stole all of their money. No one forced them to splurge on certain items. They returned to poverty because of a *poor mentality.* It is said that it is easier to take a person out of slavery than to take the slavery out of him. Nothing changes about us until our mind changes and create a new belief system. You are what you believe.

What Shapes Our Beliefs

When we are born, we know very little except how to cry. Nevertheless, we take in information through the five senses God gives us. We must depend on our parents and the world around us to teach us the basics of what we need to know (how to talk, how to walk, how to hold a spoon and even what to believe). As we grow older, we are still influenced by those around us. We hear what our parents say to us, and whatever they say, good or bad, will take root in us and shape our belief system.

Parents are powerful. A parent can shape a child to believe that he is smart or stupid, of great worth or worthless, beautiful or ugly. Our intake gets more complex as we grow older, because of friends, media, activities, mentors and external influences.

All these facets shape our beliefs. Our experiences, both positive and negative, shape our belief system. For example, if a man had a negative experience in a relationship and his heart was broken, you might hear him say, "I'll never trust another woman."

The same principle applies to women with a belief system encased in fear because of bad experiences. When they enter another love relationship, insecurities are made known because of past negative experiences that created a core belief system of mistrust and lack of faith in people.

Belief systems are generational. A prejudiced parent will pass on that belief system to their children. If a negative belief system was shaped by words and actions, then it can only be reshaped by more powerful words and actions. If a belief system was shaped over a period of time, then it will not change overnight. It will take another period of time to reshape that belief system and create a new one.

Religion also shapes our belief system. In the next chapter, we will discuss the Christian belief system, or the Christian faith.

Ten

THE CHRISTIAN FAITH

"Believe in the Lord Jesus, and you will be saved—you and your household" (Acts 16:31).

A Christian belief system is shaped from a biblical view versus a world view. We believe that the Bible is God's inspired word. We believe that there are two realms existing: the natural (physical) and the supernatural (spiritual).

Some believe that the spirit creates and births the physical. Events, circumstances, lives and influences are birthed first in the spiritual realm and then manifested in the physical realm. We existed in the spiritual realm before we were manifested here on earth. We existed in the mind of God—that's spiritual and supernatural. We were an idea, a thought and a desire of God before we were born.

We believe that we are spirit beings with souls (mind, will, emotion, and conscience) and live in physical bodies. We are spiritual and physical. We believe that when a body dies the spirit lives forever. We believe that Jesus Christ is the Son of God. He was born through a virgin, crucified to take away the sin of the world, resurrected on the third day after his death, and is now seated at God's right hand in heaven. We believe that there are three kingdoms: The Kingdom of God with God as King; a Kingdom of darkness (evil) with Satan as its ruler, and a

Kingdom of Mankind with rulers of our world—government leaders of nations.

We believe that when we believe in Jesus Christ as our personal Saviour and He becomes Lord and Overseer of our lives, then we enter into the Kingdom of God. We live on earth in the kingdom of mankind, but we also operate spiritually in the Kingdom of God. We have access to supernatural power, provision and protection. We join the family of God with God as our Father, Jesus Christ as our Saviour, and the Holy Spirit as the One who lives inside of us as our internal Guide, Teacher and Power.

BELIEVE IN GOD'S SUPERNATURAL POWER

A man in the crowd answered, "Teacher, I brought you my son, who is possessed by a spirit that has robbed him of speech. Whenever it seizes him, it throws him to the ground. He foams at the mouth, gnashes his teeth and becomes rigid. I asked your disciples to drive out the spirit, but they could not." "O unbelieving generation," Jesus replied, "how long shall I stay with you? How long shall I put up with you?" (Mark 9:17-19).

Jesus was disappointed in hearing that His disciples could not cast out the demon because of their *unbelief.* They were men who walked and talked with God every day. They saw the miracles He performed, ate the bread He multiplied, saw the blind eyes opened and the lame walking—but they doubted that they, too, had the same power within them, and that is why that power was dormant on that very day. With their lips they believed, but in their hearts they doubted.

So they brought him. When the spirit saw Jesus, it immediately threw the boy into a convulsion. He fell to the ground and rolled around, foaming at the mouth. Jesus asked the boy's father, "How long has he been like this?" "From childhood," he answered. "It has often thrown him into fire or water to kill him. But if you can do anything, take pity on us and help us." "'If you can?" said Jesus. "Everything is possible for him who believes" (Mark 9:20-23).

God's supernatural power is not a matter of "if"; it is a matter of belief. His power exists whether we believe in it or not but is activated when we believe. Sometimes we try to believe God for some things but not everything. This limits what He can do for us.

If you believe in God, then you must believe Him in everything. You must eradicate any and all doubts that He can do what He says and rest in the knowledge of His supernatural power.

"Immediately the boy's father exclaimed, 'I do believe; help me overcome my unbelief'" (Mark 9:24). In times of crises, you can take even a little faith and reach out to God for strength. Here, the father was wise in that he asked God to help him overcome any unbelief. The faith that he did have was rewarded when his son was delivered. He dared to believe, for his child's sake.

When Jesus saw that a crowd was running to the scene, he rebuked the evil spirit. "You deaf and mute spirit," he said, "I command you, come out of him and never enter him again." The spirit shrieked, convulsed him violently and came out. The boy looked so much like a corpse that many said, "He's dead." But Jesus took him by the hand and lifted him to his feet, and he stood up (Mark 9:25-27).

In the same way, you can believe for your children. You can pray and believe for them, even when they are acting rebellious. You have to pray for your children and, in praying, believe that God hears and will answer your prayers.

BELIEVE GOD'S SUPERNATURAL POWER IS IN YOU

Believe in the power within. Paul described the power that is working in us in Ephesians 3:20: *"Now to him who is able to do immeasurably more than all we ask or imagine, according to his power that is at work within us."* As a believer, you have power within you. Your faith in God makes His power reside in you. God's Holy Spirit lives inside you. That power is more than you can ask or imagine. You must believe that you are wise, you are strong, you are powerful, and you have the ability to receive miracles and to help others. The power that works within you is a power of faith that releases the power of God.

You therefore have the power to change circumstances around you. Praying is essential, which we will discuss. But beyond prayer, you also have the ability to effect change by the things you say, your attitude and the things you do. Even as faith without works is dead so is prayer without faith.

Animals act on instinct and respond to the environment around them. We have the power to *change* the environment around us to respond to us! Animals cannot invent, but we can. That is power, the power of imagination. If you believe that you are powerless, you will achieve nothing as you will nullify your ability to create.

The precious Holy Spirit is within you, and therefore you have the ability of discernment. That's power! You can discern a person's spirit and personal agenda. This is great power when you have to make crucial decisions. Imagine having the ability to know beforehand whether you should establish a joint partnership with someone before you sign the deal! Jesus said, *"But when he, the Spirit of truth, comes, he will guide you into all truth"* (John 16:13). God wants to lead you into truth regarding every single area of your life. He wants to reveal to you the truth about yourself, your relationships, your family, your business, your job, your ideas and your potential.

In Mark chapter 11 Jesus demonstrated to the disciples how to use their power within:

> *The next day as they were leaving Bethany, Jesus was hungry.*
> *Seeing in the distance a fig tree in leaf, he went to find out*
> *if it had any fruit. When he reached it, he found nothing but*

leaves, because it was not the season for figs. Then he said to the tree, "May no one ever eat fruit from you again." And his disciples heard him say it (Mark 11:12-14).

Jesus spoke to a barren tree as an illustration to His disciples. If the tree was not good for fruit, then it was good as a teaching lesson. He spoke to the tree, and it dried up from the root by the next day. The disciples were amazed. *"In the morning, as they went along, they saw the fig tree withered from the roots. Peter remembered and said to Jesus, 'Rabbi, look! The fig tree you cursed has withered!"* (Mark 11:20-21). Peter and his disciples were amazed at the power displayed by Jesus Christ even over nature. This was the illustration for His teaching on the Law of Creation—you can have what you say.

Jesus encouraged their faith. He told them that all things are possible if they believe. They too could speak to mountains (obstacles) and say, *"Go, throw yourself into the sea"* and it would happen as they said and believed. Jesus was rearranging their belief system.

In our world, we live in the natural while totally ignoring the spiritual. We do not know how powerful we are to create our world by what we say. Jesus was mentoring His disciples to think spiritually and believe for the supernatural.

In fact, this was not the first time Jesus did something supernaturally and then encouraged His disciples to do the same. He called to Peter to step out of the boat and walk on water just as He did (Matthew 14:29).

Jesus was a great coach, who demonstrated His power and used miracles and illustrations to teach and to change the disciples' belief system from religious thinking to active faith in relationship to the All Powerful God, who was able to do great things in and through them.

God wants you to change the way you think every day to reflect a belief system nurtured by His truth and Spirit. This is called inner transformation. God wants you to rule by the spirit even though you live in the natural.

You are encouraged to be strong in your spirit: *"Finally, be strong in the Lord and in his mighty power"* (Ephesians 6:10). As your spirit becomes connected to and nurtured by the Spirit of God within, you will grow in inner strength. Your faith will grow. You will grow in wisdom, power, love and peace. This is all inner strength.

Your belief system will change as you know God more and more with an ambition to be more and more like Him. You will gain the ability to create your world by what you believe, say and therefore do.

Eleven

CHANGING YOUR BELIEF SYSTEM

Do not conform any longer to the pattern of this world, but be transformed by the renewing of your mind (Romans 12:2).

The hardest thing to change is the human mind. That is why in the above verse we are admonished to be changed by renewing a process, the way we think.

FAUSTINA'S STORY

Faustina's family members had emigrated from South America to Guyana. For three generations, no one in her family owned property. Her grandparents and parents had always rented properties. They were poor in South America and continued in poverty in Guyana. A change in country did not change their belief system or their outcome. They continued as they believed. Faustina came to Canada with the same belief system, and after a failed marriage she had no desire or thought of owning a home. She was a single mother looking after her son. Her ambition was limited to survival for her and her son.

After hearing the teaching over and over that owning property will give you power and influence and that the power is yours if you believe, Faustina started to believe that with God all things are possible. She resisted the belief system of her family and created her own as a believer in God's Word. She applied the principles of The Ultimate Secret. She began to speak faith and create her new world.

Faustina's *faith* was in God as her source. She dared to dream, she dared to believe and she began to speak her dream. She *asked* God to break the generational cycle of poverty in her life. She *believed* that with God's help she would one day own her own home. She confessed, "I am saving for my home, which I will soon be able to purchase." She became a risk-taker instead of a safe-sorrier. She later received a beautiful two-bedroom home, which she declared as her first property to develop equity for leverage to acquire investment properties. Faustina became what she believed. She will not stop with one home, for now with the Law of Creation she has unlimited access to supernatural power to make impossibilities become realities.

How do you change your belief system?

CHANGE YOUR INFORMATION SOURCE

Faith comes and grows by *hearing* truth and the Word of God repeatedly. Doubt comes by *hearing* the voice of Satan or negative influences repeatedly. To change your belief, change what you listen to and hear.

The enemy speaks in various ways, through media, people, family and friends. God speaks through His Spirit and His Word as well as through media, people, family and friends. Reading the Word of God aloud is good, because it allows you to hear what you say. As you read and hear the words, they will enter your mind and create a belief system of truth. So be sure to listen to information sources that are credible and positive.

THE COMPANY YOU KEEP INFLUENCES YOUR BELIEF SYSTEM

I often say to our young people, "Show me your friends and I will show you your future." It's true. Your company indicates the type of person you are, what you believe in and what you will become. The Bible puts it this way: *"Bad company corrupts good character"* (1 Corinthians 15:33). If you want to change the way you think, you must first look at the people you constantly hang around with. Friends have powerful influence and can cause you to adopt habits and patterns of thinking by association.

This principle does not only apply to your peers and colleagues. Who are your mentors? Who are the people you look up to? Who do you model yourself after? It is wisdom to have suitable mentors. Most successful people have one or several mentors. You can even have mentors in various areas, such as spiritual, financial, physical, marriage, parenting or entertaining. In order to improve your thinking pattern and shape a healthy belief system, you must carefully choose to improve your information sources and influences.

A NEW BELIEF

When you enter the kingdom of God, your spirit is renewed, but your soul has some catching up to do. The soul includes your mind, will, emotions and conscience. Your mind influences your will, your emotions and your conscience, so your mind must be renewed.

If you once were prejudiced towards a particular race, that would not automatically change when you enter the kingdom of God. If each time you saw someone of that race and associated that person with the Ku Klux Clan, the mafia or drug dealers and judged him as inferior or superior, you will be tempted to think the same even after you become a child of God. Your mind has to be renewed. This can only be done through submitting your mind to Christ and His Word until it becomes your present truth. His Word and His spiritual influence will reshape your belief, and you will begin to love people regardless of their colour or past mistakes.

Where you are today is what you believed in the past. Change in your future necessitates a change in your mind. Your tomorrow will be determined by how you think today. Every day, you must commit yourself to having your mind renewed, thereby opening doors and opportunities that otherwise would have remained closed to you. God can help you, but you have to believe that He can.

The ultimate secret is a powerful revelation that will give you the tools to change your life and make your dream a reality. Let us rethink the various facets of our lives in which our belief system should be renewed and strengthened:

* Believe in God's supernatural power.
* Believe in your power.
* Believe for your family.
* Believe for healthy relationships and great mentors.
* Believe for a healthy mind.
* Believe in your ability to create your new world.

Pray this prayer with me:

Father God, I thank you for your Word, which is living and active in my heart today. Father, you have seen where I have been hurt, doubted, and need Your supernatural power to work in my life. Lord, I commit today to believing You, trusting You and holding on to the faith I have in you. I commit my mind to You, to be renewed, and ask that You will send the right information sources into my life so I can be transformed into Your likeness. Lord, I ask that You will give me a healthy belief system and teach me the right way of thinking regarding relationships, my family, my career, my physical and spiritual life, my financial life, my friends and my mentors. Help me to please You with the way I think, knowing that as I think in my heart I will actually become. I believe in You. In Jesus' name, Amen.

Part Four

POWER TO CONFESS

*"If you confess with your mouth, "Jesus is Lord,"
and believe in your heart that God raised him from
the dead, you will be saved. For it is with your heart
that you believe and are justified, and it is with your
mouth that you confess and are saved."*

(Romans 10:8-10)

Twelve

THE POWER TO CONFESS

The fourth principle of The Ultimate Secret is the Power to Confess. A Japanese author, Dr. Masaru Emoto, conducted research on how positive and negative thoughts toward water can affect its molecules. In one test, he filled two containers with the same type of water. Over the course of time, he spoke positive and soothing words over the first bucket of water but spoke negative, deathly words to the second container of water. He then microscopically examined the water crystals of the first bucket of water. The crystals were absolutely beautiful.

Then he examined the second bucket of water. Its water crystals were drying up and dying, shrunken from when he first poured the water into the container. The two buckets of water was filled with the same type of water, yet their contents were obviously varied. The first bucket of water was *positively* affected by Dr. Emoto's words and received *life;* the second bucket of water was *negatively* affected by his words and thus received *death*.

Similar experiments have been done with plants and animals, and it has been proven that the power of confession over things, plants, animals or people can either have a positive or negative effect. Jesus cursed the fig tree by what He said to it.

Science is a journey. In its continued search many facts have been discovered and proven that God openly reveals to us in the Bible.

The Bible is an awesome book of history, science, poetry, miracles and predictions about future events. Written in its pages is the proven truth *"The tongue has the power of life and death, and those who love it [live by it] will eat its fruit"* (Proverbs 18:21).

God and science tell us that what we *"confess"* or *"say"* can produce either life or death. Since words are so powerful, they can affect every aspect of our lives. We can bless, or curse, give life or diminish it. The Bible says,

> *Take ships as an example. Although they are so large and are driven by strong winds, they are steered by a very small rudder wherever the pilot wants to go. Likewise the tongue is a small part of the body, but it makes great boasts. Consider what a great forest is set on fire by a small spark* (James 3:4-5).

Words are so powerful that they can either free or condemn you, *"For by your words you will be acquitted, and by your words you will be condemned"* (Matthew 12:37).

Words are so powerful that what you *confess* in a court of law can set you free or bring you a sentence in prison or even the death penalty. What you *confess* is powerful.

Words are so powerful that your salvation and relationship with God is secured by what you confess: *"For it is with your heart that you believe and are justified, and it is with your mouth that you confess and are saved"* (Romans 10:10).

Words are so powerful that you can change the course of your children's lives with your repeated *confession* over their lives. Parents have the power to bless or curse their children by their *confession*. A father's confession of blessing over his child is very powerful.

Jacob, Isaac's second son, tricked his father, who was old and nearly totally blind, to get the blessing of his brother Esau, the firstborn. Isaac put his right hand on Jacob and pronounced these words:

> *"May God give you of heaven's dew and of earth's richness— an abundance of grain and new wine. May nations serve you*

*and peoples bow down to you. Be lord over your brothers,
and may the sons of your mother bow down to you. May
those who curse you be cursed and those who bless you be
blessed"* (Genesis 27:28-29).

Esau was enraged when he heard that his brother had been
blessed by their father, a pronounced blessing that would
include a transfer of birthright and inheritance to the younger
son. When Esau came to his father asking for the father's blessing of his birthright, his father trembled violently, knowing
that he had already confessed the blessing upon Jacob.

Isaac was angry and disappointed when he learned that he
was tricked and powerless to reverse his confession:

*Isaac trembled violently and said, "Who was it, then, that
hunted game and brought it to me? I ate it just before you
came and I blessed him—and indeed he will be blessed!"
When Esau heard his father's words, he burst out with a loud
and bitter cry and said to his father, "Bless me—me too, my
father!" But he said, "Your brother came deceitfully and took
your blessing"* (Genesis 27:33-35).

The confession of a father's blessing could not be revoked.
When words of faith are spoken by a believer, the power of God
begins to immediately create and set in motion a determined
path. When the word of faith is released, it is compared to an
arrow released by a warrior.

*"Sons are a heritage from the LORD, children a reward from
him. Like arrows in the hands of a warrior are sons born in one's
youth"* (Psalm 127:3-4). To parent a child is to guide him, by
what you say and pray, to a predetermined path as you seek God
for his life. The opposite of this is verbal abuse, which can crush
a child's spirit and destroy his destiny. What you say, your children will become.

GOD CREATED THE UNIVERSE BY HIS CONFESSION

By the power of His confession and by the words He spoke, God created the universe in its entirety. It says in the book of Genesis, *"In the beginning God created the heavens and the earth. Now the earth was formless and empty, darkness was over the surface of the deep, and the Spirit of God was hovering over the waters. And God said, 'Let there be light,' and there was light"* (Genesis 1:1-3).

Wow! *"And God said, 'Let there be light,' and there was light."* What awesome power was released as God spoke into nothing to become something, into chaos to become cosmos, into darkness to bring light.

In Genesis chapter 1, we read the story of creation. God created light, land, seas, plants, the moon and the stars, the fish in the seas, the birds in the air and all the animals by speaking them into existence. *"And God said..."* What He confessed became a reality. He spoke the entire universe into existence.

Then God decided to create mankind. This time, however, He changed His method of creation. He did not speak us into existence. He "made" us, as seen in Genesis 1:26-28:

> *Then God said, "Let us make man in our image, in our likeness, and let them rule over the fish of the sea and the birds of the air, over the livestock, over all the earth, and over all the creatures that move along the ground." So God created man in his own image, in the image of God he created him; male and female he created them. God blessed them and said to them, "Be fruitful and increase in number; fill the earth and subdue it. Rule over the fish of the sea and the birds of the air and over every living creature that moves on the ground."*

The process had changed, and the quality of the product had changed. The earth, the plants, the vegetables, animals and all the living species of the earth were created by God through His confession and spoken word. With mankind, however, He made (formed and fashioned) us in His *image* and in His *likeness* to be like Him in His ability, nature and spirit.

Genesis 1:1 says, *"In the beginning God created the heavens and the earth."* The Hebrew word for "to create" is *bara*, which means to bring into existence something out of nothing. The Latin phrase *"creatio ex materia"* describes the scientific assumption that "Matter can neither be created nor destroyed." This is proven with water. If you boil water it becomes steam, which when condensed becomes water again. If you burn trees you form ashes— the elements of the trees.

What was created in Genesis chapter 1 was recreated by God to form different substance and living species. All life forms have basic elements in common.

WE ARE LIKE GOD

In creating man, God said in Genesis 1:26, *"Let us make man in our image, in our likeness."* The Hebrew word for "make" is *asah*, which means to make or fashion. With the created earth God would now make, design, fashion mankind with a body made of the elements of the earth and with a spirit, *like* God.

In Genesis 2:7 we read where God created a sculptured form from the soil, in the form of a human body. He then breathed His Spirit (the breath of life) into it, and it became a living person, whom God called Adam. God is the source of life. Adam, therefore, was created with the spiritual DNA of God with the potential of wisdom, power, holiness, choice and dominion to be *like* God (ruler) on Earth.

God did not choose to create us the same way He made the other living creatures. He made us special by touching and forming us with His own hands to create every fibre of our being. In doing so, He set us apart and beyond every other creature on the planet. We are essentially special in that we were made in God's *image* and His *likeness*.

Mankind is a *personal* being with the power to think, feel and make decisions. He has the ability to make moral choices and has the capacity for spiritual growth or decline. Mankind was supposed to represent God, rule the earth and create a world with God as Lord, King and Supreme Ruler. God the Creator and Owner of the earth placed mankind, His spiritual offspring, to be His sons and daughters, to grow, develop and create the world as a kingdom under God.

"Let us make man in our image, in our likeness" (Genesis 1:26). The Hebrew word for "image" is *tselem,* which means "form, image, likeness." The Hebrew word for "likeness" is *demuth,* which means "figure resembling, pattern, something resembling."

This is very exciting, as it confirms the core of The Ultimate Secret, which is: "We are made in the image of God to speak like God the word of faith and create our world!" *Like* God and in His *image,* you can create your new world by your words of confession spoken in faith. Remember the four principles already revealed: *Have Faith, Ask, Believe, Confess.* Now you are ready to *Receive,* which is the fifth principle of The Ultimate Secret.

Mankind is the only created species with the powerful ability to speak like God and therefore create like God. Lions roar; dogs bark; sheep baa, wolves howl, birds chirp, etc—only mankind has the power to speak and create with words of faith. A parrot can be trained to imitate a person, but it cannot activate its soul to speak words of faith or words of life. You are powerful!

In Romans 10:8-11 we read,

> *But what does it say? "The word is near you; it is in your mouth and in your heart," that is, the word of faith we are proclaiming: That if you confess with your mouth, "Jesus is Lord," and believe in your heart that God raised him from the dead, you will be saved. For it is with your heart that you believe and are justified, and it is with your mouth that you confess and are saved. As the Scripture says, "Anyone who trusts in him will never be put to shame."*

Your "confession" has the powerful ability create light where there is darkness, health where there is sickness, power where there is weakness and peace where there is strife.

The ultimate secret is "We are made in the image of God to speak like God the word of faith and create our world!"

Words are so powerful that Jesus used the fig tree in Mark 11:12-24 to show the disciples how powerful their words could be, to either create or destroy. Jesus spoke to a fruitless tree, and it dried up. He then turned and said to them, *"I tell you the truth, if anyone says to this mountain, 'Go, throw yourself into the sea,' and does not doubt in his heart but believes that what he says will happen, it will be done for him."* This is incredible power and ability to remove all obstacles to our dream by what we "say." Proverbs 18:21 states, *"The tongue has the power of life and death, and those who love it will eat its fruit."*

The late American president John F. Kennedy first *declared* the goal of landing a man on the moon in May 1961. He said, "First, I believe that this nation should commit itself to achieving the goal, before this decade is out, of landing a man on the moon and returning him safely to the earth. No single space project in this period will be more impressive to mankind, or more important for the long-range exploration of space; and none will be so difficult or expensive to accomplish."

On July 20, 1969, eight years after Kennedy *said* it, Neil Armstrong and Buzz Aldrin landed on the moon in the lunar module Eagle. Mr. Aldrin, after they had safely landed, relayed this message to the control centre: "This is the LM pilot. I'd like to take this opportunity to ask every person listening in, whoever and wherever they may be, to pause for a moment and contemplate the events of the past few hours and to give thanks in his or her own way." He took communion privately and thanked God for their safe landing and the historic event. On July 21, Neil Armstrong set foot on the moon and said, "That's one small step for man, one giant leap for mankind." He and

Buzz Aldrin were the first two men to land on the moon just as Kennedy *said*.

The Wright brothers said, "We will fly." They did. What you say, you can see. You can create your new world of dreams, desires and future accomplishments. Your world in this world is up to you!

PAT'S POINTS

* You have the ability to create your world.
* You can *say* it to *see* it.
* You are made in the image of God with His spiritual DNA.
* You are made in the likeness of God to be like Him and create your world by what you *say*.
* You are special, and you were created to be like God.

Thirteen

CREATE YOUR WORLD

Speech is power. Speech is to persuade, to convert, to compel.

Ralph Waldo Emerson

In the previous chapter, we discussed how you can create your world by what you say, in the same way that God created the universe by what He said. In order to speak what you believe, you must first believe what you speak. You must believe what you are saying. If you are not convinced of what you say, no one else will be. The first principle of The Ultimate Secret is *faith*.

The Bible tells the story of a Roman centurion, in a town called Capernaum, whose servant was sick.

When Jesus had entered Capernaum, a centurion came to him, asking for help. "Lord," he said, "my servant lies at home paralyzed and in terrible suffering." Jesus said to him, "I will go and heal him." The centurion replied, "Lord, I do not deserve to have you come under my roof. But just say the word, and my servant will be healed."... When Jesus heard this, he was astonished and said to those following him, "I tell you the truth, I have not found anyone in Israel with such great faith" (Matthew 8:5-10).

This man was amazing. He had revelation on the power of spoken words of faith—the power of confession. He must have known that Jesus Christ was actually the Creator, with one of His names being the "Living Word."

In the New Testament book of John, we read about God with His Son, Jesus Christ, before the universe was created. *"In the beginning was the Word, and the Word was with God, and the Word was God. He was with God in the beginning"* (John 1:1-2). God is and was the beginning.

It also describes Mary's virginal conception of Jesus, when He entered her womb and took on flesh to become a man and live temporarily on the earth to confront evil and conquer Satan as God and human. *"The Word became flesh and made his dwelling among us. We have seen his glory, the glory of the One and Only, who came from the Father, full of grace and truth"* (John 1:14). With the triumphant resurrection of Jesus Christ after His death on the cross, we now as humans have the power to conquer evil by His power within and by the power of our words.

Jesus, who created the universe by what He said, could surely heal a man by what He said. The centurion knew that when he was in the presence of Jesus Christ, he was actually in the Presence of our Creator. Jesus was very impressed with this man's great faith. We see here not only the power of the "spoken" word but also the power of the "sent" word. *"The centurion replied, 'Lord, I do not deserve to have you come under my roof. But just say the word, and my servant will be healed.'"* Psalm 107:20 says, *"He sent forth his word and healed them."*

This is a powerful revelation, because it means you can pray for your loved ones even when they are not present, and your words of faith can touch them wherever they are around the world. You can by faith send a word of faith like an email into the spirit world to create as you say.

There is also the story in Mark 7:24-30 of a woman whose daughter was demon possessed. She came to Jesus, and she *asked* for her daughter's deliverance. Jesus sent the word of healing, and when she went home she found her daughter lying on the bed, free from the demon.

Notice The Ultimate Secret in action. Each person had *faith* in God, *asked* for a miracle, *believed, confessed* faith and *received*— have faith, ask, believe, confess and receive.

The centurion understood the power of God's spoken word. And it is God's word that healed his servant. There was a gift of healing created, inspired by the faith of the centurion. With The Ultimate Secret, you can create change in your life. *Say* it and *see* it.

No word is more powerful than the Word of God. Confess the promises of God that are found in the Bible, and they will become your reality. *"For no matter how many promises God has made, they are 'Yes' in Christ. And so through him the 'Amen' is spoken by us to the glory of God"* (2 Corinthians 1:20).

The Word of God has its own anointing. You speak it, and God performs it. *Say* it and *see* it. Speak words of faith. You can change circumstances by what you *say.*

In Mark 4:35-41, the faith of the disciples was tested. Jesus and his disciples got into a boat, and He gave them a specific word that involved instruction and their destination. *"He said to his disciples, 'Let us go over to the other side'"* (Mark 4:35). After they launched off in the boat, a furious storm arose, and the disciples were terrified. Jesus slept. He had left them in charge. He had taught them The Ultimate Secret, shown them on numerous occasions how to speak like God and create their world.

Their response, however, in the middle of the crisis was to "speak negative." *"The disciples woke him and said to him, 'Teacher, don't you care if we drown?'"* (Mark 4:38). They spoke words of fear instead of words of faith. They spoke words of death instead of words of life. They spoke words of destruction instead of words of deliverance. Jesus was disappointed in them. He rebuked them for their lack of faith and their failure to speak to the storm.

Words are powerful. Be careful what you *say*. If you lose your faith in the journey and begin to confess negatively, you will have what you *say*. In the book of Exodus, Moses and the children of Israel went through many tests in their journey from slavery to establishment. They were delivered from slavery and left Egypt in a great exodus towards a land that God had promised them. They started off boldly, but during the journey fear and lack of patience caused them to become fluctuaters.

In times of need and testing, they grumbled, complained and spoke words of death. Finally God sent a warning that they were condemning themselves by their own confession: *"The LORD said to Moses and Aaron: 'How long will this wicked community grumble against me? I have heard the complaints of these grumbling Israelites. So tell them, "As surely as I live, declares the LORD, I will do to you the very things I heard you say"'"* (Numbers 14:26-28). Supernatural power can be released to perform what you *say*. To grumble and complain is to curse the process, poison the soul and hinder the progression.

The Ultimate Secret is: We are made in the image of God to speak like God the word of faith and create our world! Jesus taught and showed His disciples how to use the power of The Ultimate Secret in Mark 4 for preservation and provision. Unfortunately, in a moment of crisis, fear nullified their belief and negated their confession. They said, "We drown!" Watch what you say and confess.

Again, these disciples were fluctuaters. They started off confidently, but in the midst of the storm along the journey they saw only defeat. Jesus got up and taught them again how to create their world by what they say, *"[Jesus] got up, rebuked the wind and said to the waves, 'Quiet! Be still!' Then the wind died down and it was completely calm"* (Mark 4:39).

Notice, Jesus rebuked the wind (the source of the storm) and He spoke to the waves (the effect of the storm), and they both responded to what He *said*.

PAT'S POINTS

* You can create your world by what you *say.*
* When in the dark, do not forget what you learned in the light.
* Remember the Word of the Lord during trials.
* In the midst of the storms of life, speak faith and negate fear.
* Live by faith and not by fear.
* Watch what you *say.*
* What you *say,* you will *see.*
* Confess the promises of God daily.

Part Five

POWER TO RECEIVE

"His divine power has given us everything we need for life and godliness through our knowledge of him who called us by his own glory and goodness."

(2 Peter 1:3)

Fourteen

THE POWER TO RECEIVE

The fifth principle of The Ultimate Secret is the Power to Receive.

The Ultimate Secret is: We are made in the image of God to speak like God the word of faith and create our world! You now have all five principles of The Ultimate Secret: Have Faith, Ask, Believe, Confess and Receive.

The word *receive* is a verb. It is an action word. It is defined as: "to come into possession of; to permit to enter; to react to in a specified manner. One definition of *receive* is "to welcome or to greet." The power to receive is the ability to welcome and admit your desire into its reality. That which is spiritual must be admitted into the natural world.

For nine months, a pregnant woman prepares herself to receive a very special child. She is preparing for the entrance of her baby. Over the next nine months, she will be learning how to take care of it, especially if it is her first child. She will read many books, talk to other mothers, eat right, get plenty of rest and change her workload. Indeed, her entire life changes in preparation for the child. As her body changes she sees herself in a different light. She feels like a different woman.

There is life within her! She has not seen the life, has never spoken to the life, has never heard from the life, but she knows it's there! Closer to the delivery date she purchases a number of supplies for her baby. She prepares the room for her baby. She even prepares her family for her baby, if she has other children, making them aware that another child will soon be added to their family. Among the many items that she buys, she is sure to purchase or be given a *receiving blanket.* This is a lightweight blanket that she will use to hold her newborn baby. It is soft and is therefore tender on the baby's skin. She will also wrap the baby in this after a bath. Rarely will a mother hold her baby without using a receiving blanket. In fact, before the mother hands her baby over to a relative, she will give the relative the blanket in preparation for what she is about to do.

The *reception* of your dream is quite the same. You know that your baby (dream) is there, you can feel its life inside you, and you visualize the manifestation of it, the day when men and women will tie your name to your dream. You have heard the promises of God. You believe. You have the word of faith. Even though you have not seen your dream as yet, you believe it will be birthed healthy and strong and will bring joy to you and those around you. You have prayed for it and about it. You have spoken to it, even though you are still waiting to hear from it. And now it's just a matter of time. Nine months? I don't know. But just a matter of time!

How are you preparing to *receive* your dream or desire? What rooms do you have ready? What have you sacrificed to ensure that nothing is lacking when your dream manifests? Have you spoken about your dream to others? Have you made people aware that in a while your life is going to be changed? What have you physically done to prepare for its manifestation?

Jesus said, *"Whatever you ask for in prayer, believe that you have received it, and it will be yours"* (Mark 11:24). You have to *receive* what you are praying for in your mind and in your heart first before you can *receive* it in the natural. You must know, without a shadow of a doubt, that what you have *asked* for is yours. You must *receive* what you *ask* for by *speaking* into existence.

What is it that you are hoping for? Believe and *receive* it now. Jesus said, *"Believe that you have received it, and it will be yours."*

Do not get tired of waiting to see the manifestation. A pregnant mother has to carry the child to full term in spite of discomfort. In the natural we see that pregnancy is the time taken for a baby to grow and develop for its new world. As there is an "appointed" time for a child to be born, so there is also an "appointed" time for every dream to come true. In due season, it will give birth. Keep believing, confessing and receiving.

A delay is not a denial. It is simply a "Wait." Know that patience builds character. *"Perseverance must finish its work so that you may be mature and complete, not lacking anything"* (James 1:4). Wait on God. He has not forgotten you. Like with the pregnant woman, it is only a matter of time. Make sure your *receiving* blanket is ready.

PAT'S POINTS

* *Receive* is a verb, an action word. You must prepare the "reception" for what you believe.
* *Receive* means "to welcome." You must maintain an attitude of expectancy and warmness toward your desire.
* Receiving is only a matter of time.
* God's timing is perfect.
* The waiting time is to develop your dream.
* Believe, confess and receive.

Fifteen

APPLYING THE ULTIMATE SECRET

"Have faith in God," Jesus answered. "I tell you the truth, if anyone says to this mountain, 'Go, throw yourself into the sea,' and does not doubt in his heart but believes that what he says will happen, it will be done for him. Therefore I tell you, whatever you ask for in prayer, believe that you have received it, and it will be yours" (Mark 11:22-24).

The ultimate secret is: We are made in the image of God to speak like God the word of faith and create our world! The five principles of the ultimate secret are Have Faith, Ask, Believe, Confess and Receive.

The story of a man called "Blind Bartimaeus" shows The Ultimate Secret in action. Jesus had come into Jericho with His disciples. As usual there was a large crowd following Him. As He was leaving the city, there was a blind man sitting by the road-side, begging. When the blind man heard that Jesus was passing by he began to shout, *"Jesus, Son of David, have mercy on me!"* (Mark 10:47).

The people started to rebuke him and tried to quiet him, but he shouted even louder. *"Son of David, have mercy on me!"* (Mark 10:48). Jesus heard the man, saw his persistence and asked that he be brought to him. *"'What do you want me to do for you?' Jesus asked him. The blind man said, 'Rabbi, I want to see.' 'Go,' said Jesus, 'your faith has healed you.' Immediately he received his sight and followed Jesus"* (Mark 10:51-52). This demonstrates the keys of The Ultimate Secret in action and manifestation starting with faith.

1. Have Faith

The blind man had faith in God. He was specific about the God He prayed to. He prayed to Jesus, Son of David, the One called "the Christ." The word *Christ* means the Anointed One, The Son of God.

Peter had a download of revelation when one day He declared excitedly to Jesus, *"You are the Christ, The Son of the living God"* (Matthew 16:16). Have faith in God.

"'Go,' said Jesus, 'your faith has healed you.'" Notice that Jesus affirmed that it was the man's faith that healed him. Jesus never touched him or anointed him with oil. The blind man's faith brought the healing he *asked* for, *confessed* and *believed* for.

Faith is a powerful force. The Bible describes men and women who

> *through faith conquered kingdoms, administered justice, and gained what was promised; who shut the mouths of lions, quenched the fury of the flames, and escaped the edge of the sword; whose weakness was turned to strength; and who became powerful in battle and routed foreign armies. Women received back their dead, raised to life again. Others were tortured and refused to be released, so that they might gain a better resurrection* (Hebrews 11:33-35).

By faith this blind man ignored his discouragers, turned his weakness to strength and boldly asked, believed and received his healing.

2. Ask

His asking was specific. *"Rabbi, I want to see."* When you know what you want, you are ready for a miracle. He did not hold back. His faith was alive and specifically targeted to a specific area in his life that he had dreamed of.

Jesus encourages us to *"Ask and you will receive, and your joy will be complete"* (John 16:24). *"Ask and it will be given to you; seek and you will find; knock and the door will be opened to you. For everyone who asks receives; he who seeks finds; and to him who knocks, the door will be opened"* (Matthew 7:7-8). God is waiting to hear from you.

3. Believe

Bartimaeus *believed* that Jesus *could* and *would* heal him. He *believed* that Jesus, unlike the crowd around Him, was merciful to the poor and would not despise a beggar. His confidence in the character and power of Jesus made him boldly ask for his healing. He had a revelation of the love of Jesus even for the poor, the sick, the widows, the orphans and people at risk.

He had heard of Jesus healing the centurion's servant; working with professionals and businessmen and labourers like His disciples; healing desperate women of incurable diseases; speaking to and blessing women of different cultures like the Samaritan woman; and healing lepers, children and all kinds of people. He was convinced that Jesus loved the world, even the blind and lame. He was right. His belief made him free to ask. *"Everything is possible for him who believes"* (Mark 9:23).

4. Confess

Notice Bartimaeus' confession: *"Jesus, Son of David, have mercy on me!"* This confirmed his faith in Jesus, the promised Messiah, the seed of David. *"Does not the Scripture say that the Christ will come from David's family and from Bethlehem, the town where David lived?"* (John 7:42). Jesus Christ was the Son of God sent to world so that the world through Him might be saved.

The Bible places emphasis on our confession.

But what does it say? "The word is near you; it is in your mouth and in your heart," that is, the word of faith we are proclaiming: That if you confess with your mouth, "Jesus is Lord," and believe in your heart that God raised him from the dead, you will be saved. For it is with your heart that you believe and are justified, and it is with your mouth that you confess and are saved (Romans 10:8-10).

Not only did blind Bartimaeus receive his sight but his dignity and destiny were restored. He became a disciple of Jesus Christ. *"Immediately he received his sight and followed Jesus"* (Mark 10:52). What you *say* you will *see.*

5. Receive

"Immediately he received his sight and followed Jesus." He exercised his *faith, asked* for his healing, *believed, confessed* his confidence in Christ, the Anointed One, and *received* His miracle.

Here is a formula for miracles:

Words of faith + Actions of Faith = Miracles as You Say!

Faith plus action creates miracles. Whether it is a shout like that of blind Bartimaeus or someone pressing through the crowd to touch Jesus like the woman who had been bleeding for years, your action releases a reaction from God.

Words are the conduit through which miracles travel.

PAT'S POINTS

* Speak your miracle into existence.
* Say it and see it.
* Be persistent.
* Keep your faith alive by speaking the promises of God.
* Words of faith + Actions of Faith = Miracles as You Say.
* Ask specifically.
* Believe, confess, and receive.

Sixteen

THE MIRACULOUS CATCH

The ultimate secret is: We are made in the image of God to speak like God the word of faith and create our world! The five principles of The Ultimate Secret are Have Faith, Ask, Believe, Confess and Receive.

The ultimate secret contains the keys to seeing your dreams and desires fulfilled through the Law of Creation.

God created mankind with the ability to create, invent, design and work to produce prosperity. You are blessed by God with the spiritual DNA to succeed.

This was declared from the beginning in Genesis 1:28: *"God blessed them and said to them, 'Be fruitful and increase in number; fill the earth and subdue it. Rule over the fish of the sea and the birds of the air and over every living creature that moves on the ground.'"*

BLESSED TO BE FRUITFUL

The word *blessed* means empowered by God and commissioned to be fruitful. *Fruitful* means to be productive. With the ability to create, you can dream, design, invent and produce solutions for our world. Think of all the inventions and development of our world since Adam and Eve. We have designed and created airplanes, submarines, trains, cars, houses made of drywall or steel instead of wood, medicines, computers, etc. We are constantly creating new solutions, which is our inherent spiritual DNA. We are like God, made in His image and in His likeness to dream, create and produce. We are people of potential. No one is born stupid. Circumstances can retard growth and development, but everyone has the ability to produce according to their talent, gifting and nurturing. Not everyone learns the same way, responds the same way or develops the same way, but everyone is gifted, divinely designed and can be nurtured for their unique purpose, which is for God's glory.

BLESSED TO INCREASE

Increase speaks of growth and development. Every living organism is either growing or dying. Choose growth. You are powerful. Take a new course. Study finances. Learn a new hobby. Read more. Develop new friendships. Join a new network. Pray for a new mentor. Take a risk. Where there is no *risk,* there is no *reward.* Create.

BLESSED TO RULE YOUR WORLD

You are made in the image of God to speak like God the word of faith and create your world! Rule your world by what you *say.* Start your dream by what you *do.* You can have what you *say.* If you do not like what you *see,* adjust what you *say. "Let the weak say, 'I am strong'"* (Joel 3:10, NKJV).

CREATED TO PROSPER

God wants you to prosper. He *said* it. *"'For I know the plans I have for you,' declares the LORD, 'plans to prosper you and not to harm you, plans to give you hope and a future"* (Jeremiah 29:11). *"Beloved, I pray that you may prosper in all things and be in health, just as your soul prospers"* (3 John 2, NKJV). *"Remember the LORD your God, for it is he who gives you the ability to produce wealth, and so confirms his covenant, which he swore to your forefathers, as it is today"* (Deuteronomy 8:18). *"For you know the grace of our Lord Jesus Christ, that though he was rich, yet for your sakes he became poor, so that you through his poverty might become rich"* (2 Corinthians 8:9).

God said it. As discussed earlier, in the book of Genesis, God created the universe by what He said. Jesus healed the sick by speaking life. He calmed the storm by His spoken rebuke. He sent words of healing to the sick, and they were healed.

God has spoken words of prosperity concerning you. Believe it and receive it.

CREATED TO SUCCEED

God wants to help you to succeed. He *said* it.

"The LORD is with me; he is my helper. I will look in triumph on my enemies" (Psalm 118:7). *"He will love you and bless you and increase your numbers. He will bless the fruit of your womb, the crops of your land—your grain, new wine and oil—the calves of your herds and the lambs of your flocks in the land that he swore to your forefathers to give you"* (Deuteronomy 7:13).

Of course we are no longer in the agricultural age with farming being the main career, but God still wants to bless you in your career or business.

LAUNCH OUT INTO THE DEEP

The first disciples of Jesus through whom He developed and launch Christianity were businessmen. Some were carpenters, fishermen and accountants. The Bible tells the story of Simon Peter and his workers fishing all night with no catch. Disappointed, the men docked their boat and were washing their nets to go home when Jesus approached them to use their boat as a platform to teach the large crowd that was following him. Jesus got in the boat belonging to Simon Peter.

He got into one of the boats, the one belonging to Simon, and asked him to put out a little from shore. Then he sat down and taught the people from the boat. Then he sat down and taught the people from the boat. When he had finished speaking, he said to Simon, "Put out into deep water, and let down the nets for a catch." Simon answered, "Master, we've worked hard all night and haven't caught anything. But because you say so, I will let down the nets." When they had done so, they caught such a large number of fish that their nets began to break. So they signaled their partners in the other boat to come and help them, and they came and filled both boats so full that they began to sink (Luke 5:3-7).

PRINCIPLES OF THE MIRACULOUS CATCH

1. Invite Jesus into your boat (career or business).

When Jesus becomes your partner, He becomes your source of inspiration, financial miracles, opportunities, great connections and open doors. Declare, "Jesus, I want you in my business. Come into my life. Step into my circumstances and release a miraculous catch." It is not always easy to break new barriers in your professional life. If you have been striving on your own, welcome, *receive,* Jesus into your life and His supernatural power will change your outcome.

2. Be Open to His Leading

"I will instruct you and teach you in the way you should go; I will counsel you and watch over you" (Psalm 32:8). Peter was not sure about Jesus' counsel. As an expert fisherman he knew that the best fishing is done during the night and near the shore—definitely not out into the deep water. He was respectful and humble enough, however, to obey. *"Master, we've worked hard all night and haven't caught anything. But because you say so, I will let down the nets."* He was smart enough to realize a good risk. Jesus had *spoken.* He who created the sea in the first place could call fish to any site by what

He said. Remember, no risk will result in no reward. Be open to doing something that you have never done before. Be open to new guidance, and be willing to take a new direction. Remember that a dead end can also mean that you have to take a right or left turn. Once Jesus comes into your life, He will create the right turn.

3. Obey

Obey even when you do not understand. We are made in the image of God, but only He is all-knowing. Two thousand years ago words like *computer, Internet, software, cellular phones,* and *digital TV* did not exist. God knows all, and as your partner in your business or career He wants to reveal to you new things, new methods and new solutions.

As Mary the mother of Jesus said to the host of the wedding in Cana, Galilee, when they had run out of wine, *"Do whatever he tells you"* (John 2:5). Jesus did His first miracle. He told the servants to fill the jars with water. It sounded ridiculous, but you must remember that miracles are *naturally* impossible and not always naturally understood. Jesus turned the water into wine.

As Mary declared when she yielded herself to the miraculous conception, *"For nothing is impossible with God"* (Luke 1:37). Be open to an interruptive fresh idea that will plunge you into a new economic level. Be willing to do something you that you have never done before. It is said, "If you want something you never had, do something you have never done." What you *do* today creates your history. What you *dream* today creates your future.

Perhaps you have been working a long time, like the disciples, and are not seeing positive results. Do not give up. Use The Ultimate Secret to create your new world. God has possibilities waiting for you. Have *faith* in God. *Ask,* pray, for your desires. *Believe* again. *Confess* the outcome. *Receive* help and a miracle from God.

God wants you to operate from glory. When you hustle, you operate from luck and frustration. With God as your helper, you operate from glory. The word *glory* means that the weight of His Presence will be in you, on you and with you in everything that you do, manifesting in favour and blessings.

Promotion comes from God (Psalm 75:6). As you go to a new level of faith, God will open new doors of opportunities and promotion. A new level of faith results in a new level of receiving all that God has stored up for you.

Pray this prayer with me:

> Dear Jesus, I believe in Your word that You want me to prosper. I put my faith in You. I ask You to bless me in my career or business. I believe that I am made in Your image and likeness with the ability to dream and create my new world. I confess that I am blessed to be fruitful, productive, grow and rule my world. I say that I have the ability and will prosper. I say that my family shall be saved. I say that I have divine health. I say that I have Your peace. I receive You in my life. I thank You for being with me in all circumstances. Use me to bring glory to Your Name, for You are my Lord and my King.
>
> In Jesus' name, amen.

PAT'S POINTS

- You are created with the spiritual DNA of God.
- You are blessed to be fruitful and productive.
- You are blessed to grow and develop.
- You are blessed to rule your world by what you say.
- You are blessed to prosper.
- You are blessed to dream and create.
- Be open to the leading from God.
- Believe what God says.
- Obey what He says.
- Say it and see it.

Conclusion

THE ULTIMATE SECRET AND YOU

The ultimate secret is: We are made in the image of God to speak like God the word of faith and create our world! The five principles of The Ultimate Secret are Have Faith, Ask, Believe, Confess and Receive.

The ultimate secret contains the keys to seeing your dreams and desires fulfilled through the Law of Creation. You can now begin to create your dreams and desires by what you *say.* This is the Law of Creation.

Double power is released when you *say* what God has already *said.* He has given you a written record of His promises that you can now apply using the five principles of The Ultimate Secret:

1. Have Faith

Have faith in God. Have faith in the Name and Word of God. His Word confirms this: *"I will bow down toward your holy temple and will praise your name for your love and your faithfulness, for you have exalted above all things your name and your word"* (Psalm 138:2). Remember that whatever battles you may face, God's Name and His Word are more powerful. The cross has already conquered on your behalf. Stay in the victory of Jesus Christ. Call on His Name and trust in His Word. What He said He will do, for what He said is already done!

2. Ask

Ask God for your desires. Ask to release the power of God. God is *asking* you to *ask* Him: *"Until now you have not asked for anything in my name. Ask and you will receive, and your joy will be complete"* (John 16:24). God wants you to life a life of joy, satisfaction and peace. He said it.

God asks, *"Call to me and I will answer you and tell you great and unsearchable things you do not know"* (Jeremiah 33:3). He wants to give you information and revelation. He wants to reveal things to you that you might unaware of. He has secrets reserved for you.

3. Believe

Believe in God. Believe in His Word. Believe in His promises. Believe in His power. Jesus said, *"Everything is possible for him who believes"* (Mark 9:23). Believe for your health, wealth, salvation and peace. Belief is a choice. It is power. If you *believe*, God will give you the ability to *conceive*. What you *conceive* you can *achieve*. You have the power to believe and change your world.

4. Confess

Say it to *see* it. Rule by what you *say*. Jesus taught us, *"I tell you the truth, if anyone says to this mountain, 'Go, throw yourself into the sea,' and does not doubt in his heart but believes that what he says will happen, it will be done for him"* (Mark 11:23).

His Word confirms it again:

> *But what does it say? "The word is near you; it is in your mouth and in your heart," that is, the word of faith we are proclaiming: That if you confess with your mouth, "Jesus is Lord," and believe in your heart that God raised him from the dead, you will be saved. For it is with your heart that you believe and are justified, and it is with your mouth that you confess and are saved. As the Scripture says, "Anyone who trusts in him will never be put to shame"* (Romans 10:8-11).

Notice that the word is in your *heart* to be transferred to your *mouth* as the vehicle to create what you *say*. What you confess with your mouth you can receive.

5. Receive.

Jesus taught us, *"Therefore I tell you, whatever you ask for in prayer, believe that you have received it, and it will be yours"* (Mark 11:24). Prepare your "receiving blanket" and by faith begin to prepare for the arrival of the miracle of your dream. Create it, believe it and receive it.

RELEASE DOUBLE POWER

Create your world by confessing the Word of God and His promises to you. God said it; now you can also say it in agreement with Him. He said in His word, *"Again, I tell you that if two of you on earth agree about anything you ask for, it will be done for you by my Father in heaven. For where two or three come together in my name, there am I with them"* (Matthew 18:19-20).

Agree with God! Say what He said about you in His Word. Here are some promises from God to confess, believe and receive.

SPEAK TO YOUR HEALTH

But he was wounded for our transgressions, he was bruised for our iniquities: the chastisement of our peace was upon him; and with his stripes we are healed (Isaiah 53:5, KJV).

SPEAK TO YOUR PROVISION

My God shall supply all your need according to his riches in glory by Christ Jesus (Philippians 4:19, KJV).

SPEAK TO YOUR OPPOSITION

No weapon that is formed against thee shall prosper; and every tongue that shall rise against thee in judgment thou shalt condemn. This is the heritage of the servants of the

LORD, and their righteousness is of me, saith the LORD (Isaiah 54:17, KJV).

Speak About Your Children

From everlasting to everlasting the LORD's love is with those who fear him, and his righteousness with their children's children (Psalm 103:17).

The seed of the righteous shall be delivered (Proverbs 11:21, KJV).

Speak About Your Grandchildren

The children of your servants will live in your presence; their descendants will be established before you (Psalm 102:28).

Speak About Your Family

"Believe in the Lord Jesus, and you will be saved—you and your household" (Acts 16:31).

Speak To Your mind

For God has not given us a spirit of fear, but of power and of love and of a sound mind (2 Timothy 1:7, NKJV).

Speak To Your strength

Let the weak say, I am strong (Joel 3:10, KJV).

Speak To your Power Within

And [David] became more and more powerful, because the LORD God Almighty was with him (2 Samuel 5:10).

Speak To Your Favour

For the LORD God is a sun and shield; the LORD bestows favor and honor; no good thing does he withhold from those whose walk is blameless. O LORD Almighty, blessed is the man who trusts in you (Psalm 84:11-12).

SPEAK TO YOUR PROSPERITY

"For I know the plans I have for you," declares the LORD, "plans to prosper you and not to harm you, plans to give you hope and a future" (Jeremiah 29:11).

SPEAK TO YOUR WEALTH

"But remember the LORD your God, for it is he who gives you the ability to produce wealth, and so confirms his covenant, which he swore to your forefathers, as it is today" (Deuteronomy 8:18).

SPEAK TO NEW BEGINNINGS

"See, I am doing a new thing! Now it springs up; do you not perceive it? I am making a way in the desert and streams in the wasteland" (Isaiah 43:19).

SPEAK TO YOUR BARRENNESS

God blessed them and said to them, "Be fruitful and increase in number; fill the earth and subdue it. Rule over the fish of the sea and the birds of the air and over every living creature that moves on the ground" (Genesis 1:28).

SPEAK CONFIDENCE

I praise you because I am fearfully and wonderfully made; your works are wonderful, I know that full well (Psalm 139:14).

Create your new world using the five principles of The Ultimate Secret.

You are made in the image of God to speak like God the word of faith and create your *new* world. Using the five principles of The Ultimate Secret—Have Faith, Ask, Believe, Confess and Receive—and create your new world.

Enjoy the journey.

SCRIPTURE REFERENCES

Dedication

Psalm 139:13-14

Acknowledgements

Ecclesiastes 4:9

Preface

Genesis 1:27

Genesis 1:26

Chapter One

Mark 11:12-14

Mark 11:20-24

Chapter Two

Hebrews 11:1

Genesis 22:7, 16-17

Mark 5:24-34; 9:23

Ephesians 6:16

Hebrews 11:6

Matthew 8:5-8, 10, 13

Mark 6:1-3, 4-6

Proverbs 4:23

Ephesians 2:8-9

John 3:16

Romans 10:9-10

Chapter Three

Genesis 11:6

Hebrews 12:2

Habakkuk 2:2

Proverbs 23:7

Romans 1:21

Chapter Four

1 Timothy 2:5-6

1 John 4:8

Hebrews 13:8

Revelation 1:8

Isaiah 9:6

Revelation 19:11

Isaiah 54:8

Psalm 68:5

John 15:15

Philippians 4:19
Romans 5:8
Psalm 37:4
Genesis 17:4, 17; 18:12
Numbers 23:19
Genesis 18:10
Genesis 21:1
Luke 12:6-7
1 Kings 17:8-16
Hebrews 13:8
Acts 10:34
Exodus 3:11
Ephesians 3:20

Chapter Five

2 Corinthians 4:13
2 Timothy 1:7
Matthew 14:26-29
Matthew 14:31
1 Timothy 6:12
James 2:14-17
James 2:26
Galatians 6:7

Chapter Six

Matthew 7:7
James 4:2
Mark 11:24
James 1:5
James 5:14-15
Luke 12:48
Matthew 11:28
1 Peter 5:7
1 Kings 3:5

2 Chronicles 1:10-12
Ephesians 3:20
Matthew 21:22
John 16:23
Matthew 3:17; 17:5
John 16:23
John 16:24
Psalm 32:8
Jeremiah 33:3

Chapter Seven

John 14:13-14
John 15:7
John 16:23-24
1 John 5:14-15
John 16:24
Matthew 7:7-11
John 5:4
Matthew 4:23-25
John 5:6
John 5:7
John 5:8-9
Psalm 103:2-5
Mark 5:21-24
Mark 5:42
James 4:2-3
1 John 5:14-15

Chapter Eight

Matthew 6:9-13
Psalm 68:5
Psalm 89:26
Psalm 103:13
Psalm 20:7

Proverbs 18:10
Matthew 4:23
Ephesians 2:10
Matthew 6:10
Matthew 6:34
Philippians 4:19
John 3:16-17
Matthew 5:7
Ephesians 4:31-32
1 Corinthians 10:13
John 10:10
1 John 3:8

Chapter Nine

Hebrews 11:1
Proverbs 23:7

Chapter Ten

Acts 16:31
Mark 9:17-19
Mark 9:20-23
Mark 9:24
Mark 9:25-27
Ephesians 3:20
John 16:13
Mark 11:12-14
Mark 11:20-21
Ephesians 6:10

Chapter Eleven

Romans 12:2
1 Corinthians 15:33

Chapter Twelve

Proverbs 18:21
James 3:4-5
Matthew 12:37
Romans 10:10
Genesis 27:28-29
Genesis 27:33-35
Psalm 127:3-4
Genesis 1:1-3
Genesis 1:26-28
Genesis 1:1
Genesis 1:26
Romans 10:8-11
Mark 11:12-24
Proverbs 18:21

Chapter Thirteen

Matthew 8:5-10
John 1:1-2
John 1:14
Psalm 107:20
Mark 7:24-30
2 Corinthians 1:20
Mark 4:35
Mark 4:38
Numbers 14:26-28
Mark 4:39

Chapter Fourteen

Mark 11:24
James 1:4

Chapter Fifteen

Mark 11:22-24
Mark 10:47
Mark 10:48
Mark 10:51-52
Matthew 16:16
Hebrews 11:33-35
John 16:24
Matthew 7:7-8
Mark 9:23
John 7:42
Romans 10:8-10
Mark 10:52

Chapter Sixteen

Genesis 1:28
Joel 3:10
Jeremiah 29:11
3 John 2
Deuteronomy 8:18
2 Corinthians 8:9
Psalm 118:7
Deuteronomy 7:13
Luke 5:3-7
Psalm 32:8
John 2:5
Luke 1:37

Conclusion

Psalm 138:2
John 16:24
Jeremiah 33:3
Mark 9:23
Mark 11:23

Romans 10:8-11
Mark 11:24
Matthew 18:19-20
Isaiah 53:5
Philippians 4:19
Isaiah 54:17
Psalm 103:17
Proverbs 11:21
Psalm 102:28
Acts 16:31
2 Timothy 1:7
Joel 3:10
2 Samuel 5:10
Psalm 84:11-12
Jeremiah 29:11
Deuteronomy 8:18
Isaiah 43:19
Genesis 1:28
Psalm 139:14

About the Author

PAT FRANCIS, D-C.P.C., M.DIV., D. MIN., PH.D.

Dynamic, powerful, spiritual, visionary, an astute business professional, humanitarian, caring and understanding are just a few words to describe Pat Francis.

Dr. Pat Francis, a humanitarian, pastor, president and founder of several charities and for-profit companies. The various innovative and dynamic programs run by the charities are transforming lives and providing solutions for at risk children and youth. Dr Francis has been honored with several awards both in Canada and America for the success of the programs.

She sits on the Board of several Christian Networks and is a member of the Women Presidents Organization, an international network of women with multimillion dollar companies.

In January 2008, Dr. Francis was appointed as a United Nations Representative (NGO) with influence as a transformational activist to deal with humanitarian issues, systemic poverty in partnership with world leaders. With this appointment her goal is to break systemic poverty as she helps people to create systemic prosperity. Dr. Pat travels the world sharing her message of hope as an international conference speaker.

Her motto is "Charity and Enterprise" backed by her mantra "Prosperity with purpose and wealth creation for His cause." At the end of the day her personal mission to serve God, serve others and make her world a better place prevails in every-thing she does.

She is an author and TV host with her weekly program "Good News with Pat Francis". www.patfrancis.org

CHARITIES

Pat Francis Ministries—www.patfrancis.org
Kingdom Covenant Ministries
Kingdom Covenant Leadership Institute
Kingdom Covenant Leadership Network
Kingdom Covenant International Fellowship
Kingdom Covenant Academy
Kingdom Covenant Collegiate (High School)
Compassion for the Nation
Acorn to Oak Community & Youth Services—
www.acorn2oak.org

BUSINESSES

Elomax—www.elomax.com
Admarie Communication Services—www.admarie.com

MEMBER ORGANIZATIONS

The International Coalition of Apostles
Women Presidents' Organization

Dr. Pat Francis' Contact Information

For additional information regarding the Pat Francis Ministries' services, please send an email to info@patfrancis.org or call toll free 1-877-668-5433 extension 2216 or 2234, Monday to Friday 9 a.m. to 5 p.m. (EST).

Canadian Head Office

Pat Francis Ministries
P.O. Box 10
Station A Toronto, Ontario M9C 4V2 Canada
Telephone: 905-566-1084
Fax: 905-566-1154
Email: info@patfrancis.org
Website: wwwpatfrancis.org

USA Distribution Center

Pat Francis Ministries
6632 Telegraph Road
Box 500
Bloomfield Hills, Michigan
48301 USA

Products Available

Books

Bloodline Sins, God promised that the sins of the parents shall fall on their children up to three generations.

God in Business is a 12 part teaching series. Each series is comprised of 4 life changing messages.

Achieving New Levels of Prosperity will help you to achieve new levels of financial prosperity as well look into ways to earn money and to make money work for you.
Includes FREE Workbook

In this series ***"Evicting Demonic Squatters"***, not only will you be set free but you will be able to help others to also obtain their freedom....

Set Free To Soar, Isaiah says, "Since ancient times no one has heard, not ear has perceived, no eye has seen any God besides you, who acts on behalf...

Telephone 1-877-668-5433 or visit www.patfrancis.org

Take time to review God's *Building Blocks for Success* each day and let God's wonderful promises be revealed in your life. 2nd Peter 1:2

Living to Leave a Legacy, will help to position you for your king-priest calling. As a king you are anointed with power, influence, wealth and wisdom...

Unleash your Power, there is a power within you that must be unleashed this year to possess your inheritance that is already preordained for you. (4 Part Series)

Anointed In the Marketplace, will help to position you for your king-priest calling. As a king you are anointed with power, influence, wealth and wisdom...

Battle for the Soul, Beloved, I can tell you that you can stand on the word of God and nothing by any means shall harm you...

Calling God Down, Isaiah says, "Since ancient times no one has heard, not ear has perceived, no eye has seen any God besides you, who acts on behalf...

Deliverance from Fear, Increasingly, the news today is inundated by stories of war and rumors of war, sickness and disease, threats and acts of violence...

Ex-Posing the Enemy, There are generational causes that can give Satan the right to you and your family. You will be able to identify family traits...

Faith The Step Before the Miracle, Faith is both a journey and a process. It begins with hope and ends in complete and total belief in what you cannot ...

God In The Workplace, Isaiah says, "Since ancient times no one has heard, not ear has perceived, no eye has seen any God besides you, who acts on behalf...

No Guts, No Glory, is a stimulating new series that will challenge you. I believe that you will see issues in your life very differently after...

Praise Him Anyhow, Beloved, I can tell you that you can stand on the word of God and nothing by any means shall harm you...

Strategic Spiritual Warfare, we have seen unmistakable images on T.V. about battles, terrorism and religious warfare. There is however , an even greater war...

The Power Of His Name, God promised that the sins of the parents shall fall on their children up to three generations. Have you noticed recurrent cycles in your family such as...

Time Seasons and Purpose, Isaiah says, "Since ancient times no one has heard, not ear has perceived, no eye has seen any God besides you, who acts on behalf...

What To Do When You Don't Know What to Do, will help to position you for your king-priest calling. As a king you are anointed with power, influence, wealth and wisdom...

VIDEO MEDIA

Title: **Anointed For Breakthrough Part 1**
Description: 2006 is the year of the breakthrough.

Title: **Designing the Dream - Part 1 of 4**
Description: Dr. Pat teaches on realizing your dreams.

Telephone 1-877-668-5433 or visit www.patfrancis.org

Title: **Praising God - How to Praise**
Description: How to praise and win God's heart

Title: **The Gift of Wisdom - A Humble Heart**
Description: How to have a humble and wise heart

Title: **The Powerful Church of our Lord Jesus Christ**
Description: The power and purpose of the Church

Title: **Unleashing your Power**
Description: Unleashing your full potential

Title: **Praise Him Anyhow**
Description: Praising through the storms of life